MW01255219

Boyd writes, "A generous life is an attractive apologetic." This is, in many ways, the theme of this special book. We are most Christlike when we are giving sacrificially. *The Power of Generosity* paints a picture of what a good and faithful steward looks like, someone who goes well beyond stewarding financial resources. In a society and culture where most of us struggle with wanting more and more of what we already have enough of, generosity stands out and causes others to notice. People easily remember experiencing surprising acts of generosity, especially when the giver gives up something of value. The pages of this book help give a clear perspective of generous living. This encouragement draws us into the adventure of being generous with all we have and all we are.

David Wills, president emeritus of the National Christian Foundation

I truly believe that mature sons and daughters desire to be led into generosity. Boyd Bailey has done just that by tackling the topic in the way only he can, with stories, revelation, and winsomeness. Boyd is an expert and not only lives out the principles in this book but eagerly desires to bring others with him. This book is a gift to the body of Christ, celebrates the power behind generosity, and challenges those of us wanting to understand that power.

Rachel Faulkner Brown, director of Never Alone Widows
and author of *Widow's Might* and *Father's House*

The Power of Generosity is unique among all the books I've read on the topic of generosity. It amplifies the truth that biblical generosity originates with love, is motivated by love, and is sustained by love and that the expression of love through generosity leads us into a life of adventure and freedom. The scriptural teachings in the book are solid truths on which to build generous lives, and the stories of generous individuals and families encourage us to step into this great adventure with our heavenly Father. *The Power of Generosity* exudes the heart of God!

Bill Williams, former president of Generous Giving,
former CEO of the National Christian Foundation,
and director of Biblical Generosity at Local Church Forsyth

Through storytelling, prayers, Scripture, quotes, poetry, and a discussion guide, Boyd has created a delightful book that will inspire and encourage us toward the healing power of generosity in a holistic way. This book is a joy to read on its own but can also be used with a study group. Practical tips are included alongside interviews with three icons known for aligning biblical principles to money: Howard Dayton, Ron Blue, and Terry Parker. You can read this book over and over since the truths are timeless and well told. It is a necessary read for any believer and a perfect gift for someone exploring what God says about generosity.

Angela Correll, author of *Restored in Tuscany*,
and **Jess Correll**, founder of First Southern National Bank

Boyd combines a masterpiece of biblical teachings, fascinating stories, and useful illustrations describing generosity principles that help us live this adventure with Jesus. As these chapters unfold, we find ourselves responding, *Yes, Lord, I want this kind of life with you.* Soon our hearts will exclaim, *Thank you, Lord, for showing me how it's possible!* This book, *The Power of Generosity*, is a wonderful resource for the spiritual journey of generosity, using reflective questions for personal and group discussion and prayer. You'll buy the first copy for yourself and then many more copies to give away. Why? Because you love being generous.

R. Thomas Ashbrook, author of *Mansions of the Heart*, *Contagious Fire*,
Presence, and *Connected*

Journey alongside Boyd Bailey in *The Power of Generosity: Experiencing God's Amazing Abundance* as he unpacks the transformative impact of biblical generosity on our lives. Through personal stories, profound biblical wisdom, prayer, and practical ways to be generous with *all* God has given you—your time, talent, treasure, relational ties, and unique personal testimony—this book is a road map to discovering greater joy, clearer purpose, and deeper relationships with God and others. In each chapter, the Holy Spirit invites, guides, and empowers you to taste and see God's abundant love, power, and transformation as you step out in faith and apply practical biblical principles of generosity to your life.

Teri Bledsoe, board member of Women Doing Well

With warmth and wisdom on every page, Boyd teaches us that we find the power of generosity first and foremost in receiving the love of God. He compellingly makes the case that generosity is about relationships, not money, and that fullness of life is experienced by those who give their lives away. If you want more joy, read this book.

Brian Grasso, cofounder and CEO of Simple Charity

May you be exceedingly and abundantly blessed as you watch God's Word come alive through examples of people living radically generous lives. I have been both inspired and encouraged on my own generosity journey. Enjoy this treasure and share it with others!

Lacie Stevens, senior partner at Generous Giving

The Power of Generosity is a profound and practical guide for believers seeking to live out God's call to a generous life. With a beautiful blend of Scripture, wisdom-filled stories, and deep discussion, this book not only inspires but also equips readers to align their hearts with God's generosity. Whether you're close to the beginning of your journey of generosity or looking to deepen your practice, this book is a resource that transforms both mind and soul.

Jeff Johns, CEO of Impact Foundation

For me, the essence and source of *The Power of Generosity* is best captured in the very first chapter, which is about the generous love of God. We cannot personally encounter God and not be generous. When reality hits and we accept that God knows and calls us each by name, that we are his, and that he loves us, life is forever transformed. This truth is foundational to this book and well laid out in the very beginning. I invite you to delve into these pages and experience the generous love of God as he leads you on your personal journey of generosity.

Lee Torrence, former managing director of IBM

True generosity isn't a transaction; it's a lifestyle. *The Power of Generosity* captures the essence of living openhandedly, showing how generosity reflects God's heart and reshapes our priorities. This is more than a book. It's a guide to experiencing the life-changing power of generosity.

Andy Stanley, founder and senior pastor of North Point Ministries

THE POWER OF GENEROSITY

EXPERIENCING GOD'S AMAZING ABUNDANCE

BOYD BAILEY

BroadStreet
PUBLISHING

BroadStreet Publishing® Group, LLC
Savage, Minnesota, USA
BroadStreetPublishing.com

The Power of Generosity: Experiencing God's Amazing Abundance

9781424569465 (hardcover)
9781424569472 (ebook)

Cover and interior by Garborg Design Works | garborgdesign.com

Printed in China

25 26 27 28 29 5 4 3 2 1

To the National Christian Foundation,
where generosity flourishes and
where all the royalties from this book will go
to be granted to Christian ministry.

Contents

Foreword

In a world where possessions often define our worth and status, Boyd Bailey's exploration of generosity founded on biblical teachings is both timely and transformative. I have had the privilege of witnessing Boyd's passion for this topic firsthand. Through our work at the National Christian Foundation (NCF), I've seen Boyd's commitment to living out generosity in his own life. It has been inspiring to all who know him. His insights are not just theoretical; they are born out of a genuine desire to see transformation and positive change in our communities through the power of generosity.

Throughout my own journey of leading others, I have come to understand the profound effect of aligning our lives with God's desires, particularly his perspective on wealth and generosity. Generosity is not merely about financial giving; it is about stewardship and the joyful responsibility of managing all that God has entrusted to us for his glory.

When I founded the NCF affiliate office in Seattle in 2007, serving as its first president and later as the president of NCF's northwest region, I had the privilege of seeing the transformation that occurs when individuals embrace the biblical truth that everything we have belongs to God. The joy that comes from freely giving, knowing it is in obedience to God's Word, is immeasurable. And as we experience the most historic transfer of wealth between generations, we see multiple generations becoming catalysts for change in their communities. Faith *can* influence and transform society, and it has been my life's most meaningful and inspirational work to be a part of it.

My firm belief is that it all starts with God's Word. Scripture reminds us that generosity is not just a good idea but a core aspect of the Christian faith. Generosity reflects God's heart for his people and his desire for us to live abundantly and generously, mirroring his own character. In these pages, Boyd connects our hearts to Scripture and the theme of generosity.

What makes Boyd's perspective particularly compelling is his ability to bridge the gap between biblical teachings and practical application. He doesn't just outline principles; he illustrates them with stories and examples that resonate with our daily lives. He challenges us to examine our priorities and to live with open hearts and hands, reflecting the love of Christ in all that we do.

As you read *The Power of Generosity*, I pray you will be inspired to embark on your own journey of generosity and that you will discover the profound joy and fulfillment that come from aligning your life with God's priorities. May you be empowered to live boldly, give generously of all that he has entrusted to you, and be inspired to embrace a life of radical generosity.

Kendra VanderMeulen

CEO, National Christian Foundation
July 2024

Preface

A Life of Generosity

My maternal grandmother, Elizabeth Anderson Goss, lived a generous life. She was not wealthy or poor. Her lifestyle reminds me of the prayer in Proverbs 30:7–9: "O God, I beg two favors from you before I die: First, help me never to tell a lie. Second, give me neither poverty nor riches! Give me just enough to satisfy my needs! For if I grow rich, I may become content without God. And if I am too poor, I may steal and thus insult God's holy name" (TLB). I don't remember a time when she wasn't generous. A few years ago, I was honored to officiate her funeral. How do you describe in twenty minutes someone whose life spanned ninety-two years and who prayerfully and intentionally blessed others? In her honor, I would like to mention a few highlights of the person who modeled for me a journey of generosity by pointing people to Jesus and giving what she had to help others.

Elizabeth Anderson was the oldest of six children (four brothers and one sister). The Anderson family lived in the country until my grandmother was about ten years old, at which point they moved to town, where her dad bought the general store. In her words, she grew up a city girl. All the children showed an interest in business, including my grandmother, who, as an adult, worked as a financial manager for a thriving regional hardware supply company.

During my eulogy of her, I recalled her opening her home for friends and family with a table laden with Southern cuisine: homemade buttermilk biscuits, fried chicken, mashed potatoes with gravy, green beans, and pecan pie, plus as much sweet tea as you could guzzle. I felt a special bond with my grandmother; she knew me, understood me, and loved me generously despite my quirks. She was unhurried when we were together, always giving me her full attention. Generosity to my grandmother was not a *have to* but a *get to*—an overflow of her love for the Lord.

Her business acumen reminds me of the Proverbs 31 woman who took care of her family while working a time-consuming job. Her entrepreneurship included a rental home she owned in a small town fifty miles away, where her brother Thomas lived. When I was twelve years old, my immediate family suffered a second divorce. My mother, with three boys in tow, struggled to buy us food and clothing, though she worked two jobs and I hustled mowing yards and washing trucks. Grandmother offered for us to stay in her rental home at no cost. What a gift to have a roof over our heads without fear of eviction. I lived in this modest house through middle and high school. I walked to school and walked to town to run errands. Grandmother's generosity gave us peace of mind and physical safety and security.

However, the best gift Grandmother gave our family was her generous prayers. Many times in our conversations, she would remind me to pray and trust the Lord. I did pray, but I prayed as someone seeking the Lord, not as someone who knew the Lord. Grandmother's generous prayers for my soul's salvation were answered in the spring of my freshman year of college. By God's grace, I placed my total trust and faith in Jesus Christ as my Lord and Savior.

Grandmother encouraged me to read and study the Bible so my faith would be grounded in God's Word. She gave me my grandfather's Bible with an inscription on the first page: "To my grandson Boyd a beloved son in whom the Lord is well pleased." After college graduation, I attended seminary (theological graduate school). During this season, she ensured that my shoes looked nice. She liked buying me shoes. This was her logic: "Son, since you bring with you the good news of Jesus Christ, it's important you wear good-looking shoes."

Grandmother was generous to the very end of her life, when she gave me the gift of officiating her funeral and asked me to carry on her legacy of generous living. The spirit of this book is the spirit of a generous grandmother who lavishly loved me and those who were blessed to ever be in her presence.

I love you, Grandmother, and my shoes are looking good!

Prologue

Experiencing the Faith Adventure of Generous Living

Following Jesus is an adventure in which we are sometimes confused but never bored. Ask the disciples. I promised my wife, Rita, right after I became a Christian and right before we were married, "If you marry me, you will never be bored." Many years later, she reminds me that I underpromised and overdelivered.

Our faith adventure of following Jesus takes us into the unknown. And the unknown, while illumined by God's glory, may be the hardest part of our journey of generosity. *How will our needs be met? What is God's part? What is my part?* Gratefully and not surprisingly, the Lord has exceeded our needs and expectations throughout our journey into the glorious unknown. Following Jesus into the unknown is where he has made himself most known to us in a loving, intimate relationship. The faith adventure of generous living has become our rich opportunity to be known and loved by God more deeply.

As Jesus taught, freedom and fulfillment come only by giving our lives away: "If you cling to your life, you will lose it; but if you give up your life for me, you will find it" (Matthew 10:39 NLT). At this crossroads of giving our lives away for him, we have discovered the abundant life he has for us. A life that is truly life.

The heart of this book is for you to experience a deeper relationship with the Lord and others as you take the step of faith by following him in the great adventure of giving away your life.

One of the joys I have in serving as the Georgia president of the National Christian Foundation (NCF) is meeting families who, by God's grace, are living out generous giving at home, at work, in their community, and at church. One of these special couples is Jonathan and Callie Rich. Two of our daughters,

Bethany and Anna, have worked for the Riches and have seen up close their generous lives. Our NCF communications team creatively captured their story, so there is no better way to begin this book than to be inspired and instructed by a young couple who is experiencing their great adventure of following Jesus through the power of generous living. Meet the Riches:

> Jonathan and Callie Rich have their hands full. With seven young children and a growing real estate business to run, you'd think that they wouldn't have much time to think strategically about giving. But with their Giving Fund (also known as a donor-advised fund), they're able to build strategic generosity through their business. In the process, J. Rich Atlanta and their clients are helping everyone from adoptive families to thirsty Ethiopian villagers and Syrian refugees to lead full lives, too.
>
> While their days are vibrant and fulfilling today, daily life a decade ago was very different. At 25 years old, Jonathan found himself struggling with an undiagnosed autoimmune disorder, which hit him worst right when their first son was born. Jonathan says, "I was short of breath and could barely get out of bed. I was having hallucinations, blurry vision, and my knees were so swollen that I couldn't even bend them." He tried all types of conventional and alternative treatments with no results.
>
> Finally, after five years of suffering, a friend led him to a new doctor and he finally found a treatment that put the disease in remission. Callie says, "That was by far the hardest journey that we've been on. We only got through it by putting one foot in front of the other, one day at a time."
>
> Perhaps it was this challenging ordeal that strengthened the Rich's resolve to pursue a life of purpose. Jonathan says, "Real estate is our career at this season in our life, but really it's just a vehicle for the purpose and impact that we are trying to create in our neighborhood, our community, and in our city."
>
> Jonathan and Callie live and work in Atlanta's diverse, intown, Kirkwood neighborhood, where the office of J. Rich Atlanta is housed in a bungalow right next door. They believe investing in their community is integral to their faith. "The church is not an evangelical gathering that happens on Sunday morning," Jonathan says. "The church is a

community of believers who are gathering together, and then trying to encourage and develop the community around them. As Christians, community is where we live. The work that we do, in the place that we live, is really important. Where we choose to live matters."

The Riches have seven children, four of whom are adopted. Callie, a former labor and delivery nurse, says, "After our first son was born, the Lord put adoption on our hearts. We adopted our first daughter, and it was such a humbling, beautiful journey that we knew it would become a larger thread in the fabric of our family's story. We became large advocates of adoption, and it's a cause we love to champion within our community."

"I remember a huge turning point for us was when we realized that if we were really pro-life, we must also necessarily be pro-adoption. Not everyone is called to adopt. But if you come from the perspective that all life is valuable, then you need to be willing to participate in the nurturing and care for that life when it comes," Jonathan adds. "The bottom line is we realized that we couldn't sell enough houses, give away enough money, or build an organization that would have any greater impact than just being good parents."

"Teaching our kids to love the Lord, love the church, and love each other is the primary work we are called to do," says Callie.

While their passion for adoption led to a personal love for giving toward others' adoptions, they decided to focus their business giving on four causes. "The causes that we want to anchor the story we are telling are: the thirsty, the fatherless, the homeless, and the underserved," Callie says.

These goals inspired them to support underserved youth through educational programming with both the East Lake Foundation and Ron Clark Academy. Charity: Water is also a long-term partner, and J. Rich Atlanta has helped build three large water wells in Ethiopia that serve almost 600 people each. They also partnered with Preemptive Love Coalition to help rebuild some of the first homes in Aleppo, Syria, for returning refugees.

But they want to do more. "Our hope is to leverage our influence and impact with our clients and within the real estate community to connect others to the good work these organizations are doing," Callie says. "It is about giving the money, but it's also about helping others to engage with charitable organizations that are doing really good work. We say it's an invitation into the stories of those making life brighter."

The National Christian Foundation (NCF) enables them to do that. "We were first introduced to NCF through our financial planners, who recommended that we open a Giving Fund to simplify our personal giving," explains Callie.

"When we looked at options for our business giving model, we realized that we didn't want to start our own foundation. We really just wanted to give money to organizations that were already doing really good work. NCF was the best choice to help us do that with transparency, simplicity, and a good level of accountability. All of the partners that we wanted to recommend grants to were available to us through NCF. So, we opened an account at NCF, and called it the Brilliant Fund."

As a company, J. Rich Atlanta gives 10 percent of their revenue to the Brilliant Fund. From there, they recommend grants quarterly to charitable partners they've identified. Then, they share those partners with their clients and try to connect them with the good work being done by those charities. Some of their clients have never given to a charity before.

The Brilliant Fund gives J. Rich Atlanta a way to help their clients experience the gift of generosity. Jonathan says, "It's exciting to say, 'because you purchased or sold a home with us, you got to participate in this bigger story.' Our ultimate goal is that there would be a ripple effect, and in the next five years, our clients will get personally involved in the organizations that we support."

Callie adds, "We work to identify a quantifiable result with the funds granted, so we can very specifically say to our clients, you were able to provide 200 reusable diapers to babies in Haiti, or you were able to provide clean water to 600 people through the creation of a well. We hope to inspire our clients and our community about the possibilities for making an impact."

Last year, a couple bought a house with J. Rich Atlanta while the company was supporting Preemptive Love Coalition in Syria. Jonathan says, "Our clients knew about Preemptive Love, and they were blown away, because they would have never been able to give the amount of money that was given through Brilliant as part of the

> home-buying process. They were so happy that they got to participate in such a significant way."
>
> Over the next 10 years, J. Rich Atlanta has set a goal to give away at least $2 million. But Jonathan and Callie are quick to add that monetary goals and metrics are not the measure of their success. Callie sums it up this way: "We never set out to have an influential business or a large family. I think it's come down to simple obedience—just putting one foot in front of the other and letting the Lord tell a story that is bigger than us."[1]

The Riches model an imperfect family following their perfect heavenly Father in the great adventure of giving their lives away relationally, vocationally, spiritually, and financially.

Where the Power of Generous Living Originates

In my journey of generosity, I have been inspired by genuine examples in various forms, which allowed me to be me and not to try to compete by outgiving somebody else. God's Word and the Holy Spirit have also instructed me about why I have the privilege to be generous: because of the radical generosity of my heavenly Father's example and out of my heartfelt gratitude for the gift of his Son, Jesus Christ, and all his other abundant graces.

The power of generous living originates in the all-powerful One—God the Father, Son, and Spirit. In him is power to save, forgive, and energize to serve. Power to physically or emotionally heal or mend a relationship. Power to give wisdom to the humble and purpose to his beloved children. The Father, Son, and Spirit have enriched us in every way so we can be generous in every way. My prayer is for all of us to experience God's powerful love by his working through our generous lives.

May I echo Paul's words to the Ephesians: "Remembering you in my prayers, that the God of our Lord Jesus Christ, the Father of glory, may give you the Spirit of wisdom and of revelation in the knowledge of him…and what is the immeasurable greatness of his power toward us who believe, according to the working of his great might that he worked in Christ when he raised him from the dead

1 "This Family Uses Their Business and Their Giving Fund to Share Generosity with Others," National Christian Foundation, January 13, 2021, https://www.ncfgiving.com.

and seated him at his right hand in the heavenly places" (Ephesians 1:16–17, 19–20 ESV).

Grateful to my generous Savior, Jesus Christ,

Boyd Bailey

Roswell, GA

Introduction

With the goodness of God to desire our highest welfare, the wisdom of God to plan it, and the power of God to achieve it, what do we lack?[2]

A. W. Tozer

We want you to know about the grace that God has given the Macedonian churches.... They gave themselves first of all to the Lord.... See that you also excel in this grace of giving.

2 Corinthians 8:1, 5, 7 NIV

God does not need your money, but he does want you. With generous love, Jesus Christ gave himself for you. As you receive God's gift of grace, God calls you to generously give yourself to him to be loved and to love. You first give yourself to the Lord since he has given his all for you.

Generosity for followers of Jesus Christ begins with your heavenly Father's gift of his Son. Once you receive Jesus as your Savior and Lord, you give your life as a living sacrifice of praise and worship to God. When the Lord has you, he has all of you: your relationships, your resources, and anything you would be tempted to say you own. You are a custodian, not an owner. You are in the honored role of caring for God's blessings in your life in a manner that blesses other lives. The grace of giving compels you toward a lifetime journey of generous living.

The Grace of Giving: A Compelling Example

The church of Macedonia, referenced in 2 Corinthians 8, was poor in material means but rich in generosity. Out of great joy, they gave "beyond their means" (v. 3 ESV). Instead of restricting themselves to giving only a certain percentage, they were freed by grace for generous living. Paul illustrated to the more prosperous Corinthian church that generosity was a matter of first giving themselves. He attempted to motivate this abundantly resourced group of believers to cheerfully give to Christ's work by sharing with them stories of Christians who

2 A. W. Tozer, *The Knowledge of the Holy* (HarperOne, 1961), 64.

gave aggressively out of their extreme poverty and severe trials. Joyful generosity can mean more to those who have less. It may mean more to the poor because they give sacrificially, not out of abundance. Generous living is not just a mere transaction but a mighty transformation, starting with the gift of your life to the Lord. A community of believers or individual Christians who experience the riches of God's grace joyfully can excel in the grace of giving.

The spirit of the grace of giving is not that we *have to* give but that we *get to* give. It's a privilege. So what is the grace of giving, and why do we need this grace of giving? The grace of giving is God's gift to a humble heart to freely give, empowering us to model the way of Jesus. God gives grace to the humble who acknowledge their dependence on him. Because the Macedonian church had received God's grace, they were empowered to willingly and freely give. Their generosity flowed from a life that grace had freed from the shackles of guilt and greed. Even today the followers of Jesus Christ in this eastern European region beautifully live a legacy of generosity.

Modern Macedonians

In my early thirties, I experienced a great adventure when I traveled to Macedonia (today officially North Macedonia) on three occasions to provide leadership training for university students. The generous hospitality of the local gathering of Jesus followers was warm and inviting. Conversations over Turkish coffee in the mornings and extended discussions over appetizing, unhurried dinners helped me immerse myself in the culture and better understand how to love and serve my Macedonian brothers and sisters in Christ. Their grace in giving to me and our team flowed out of resources inferior to most Americans but with resourcefulness and eternal impact. These Jesus lovers did more with less because of the grace of God overflowing through their generosity. Their grace of giving excelled for God's glory.

Excel in the Grace of Giving

After affirming the modest Macedonian church as a model of inspiration for the believers in Corinth and instructing the Corinthians to follow their example of generosity, Paul affirmed the Corinthians for their faith, speech, knowledge, diligence, and love. But the Apostle said, in essence, that the one thing they lacked as full-fledged disciples of Jesus was to "excel in this grace of giving" (2

Corinthians 8:7 NIV). They were a good church, but to become a great church, Paul commanded them to create a compelling culture of generosity that would meet the needs of believers and extend the same love and hospitality to unbelievers. The Lord wants believers to celebrate generous giving.

A generous life is an attractive apologetic (which in theological terms means a defense of the authenticity of Christianity) that draws seeking hearts to a clearer understanding of God's gospel.

Here are some ways we can excel in the grace of giving:

- **Be Intentionally Prayerful:** Intentionality in prayer plays a crucial role. As an authentic follower of Jesus, prayerfully consider your giving, seeking guidance from God to discern how you can contribute meaningfully. This intentional approach aligns with the Lord's heart, which highlights the significance of a cheerful and purposeful heart in the act of giving.
- **Be Freely Generous:** Scripture emphasizes generosity, another essential aspect, throughout its pages. Proverbs 11:25 promises, "A generous person will prosper; whoever refreshes others will be refreshed" (NIV). Practically, this means cultivating a mindset of abundance rather than scarcity and recognizing that God blesses you to be a blessing to others. Generosity extends beyond monetary gifts and encompasses sharing time, expertise, relationships, and resources with those in need.
- **Be Disciplined in Consistency:** Consistency is also vital to excelling in the grace of giving. Regular, committed giving reflects a steadfast dedication to supporting others and God's work. Malachi 3:10 encourages us to consistently bring our tithes, trusting in God's promise to open the windows of heaven and pour out blessings. Discipline is essential to being a dependable disciple of your generous Jesus.
- **Be Pervasive in Love:** Loving with a heart of compassion and empathy is crucial to excelling in the grace of giving. Jesus Christ exemplified this through his compassionate acts, urging believers to show kindness and mercy. Engaging with the needs of others on a personal level fosters a deeper connection and understanding of the impact one's generosity can have on individuals and communities.

The Goal of This Book

The goal of this book is freedom, not guilt; joy, not dread; love, not fear. The power of generous living rests in the power of God. So our part is to abide in Christ and trust him to grow our abundant life, an abundant life that experiences the true riches of being fully known and fully loved so that we are available for others to be fully known and fully loved. Financial prosperity may or may not come, but either way, the promise of generosity is that we will refresh others and, in the process, be refreshed.

Here is a helpful prayer for us as we join together in our adventure of generosity.

A Liturgy for Generosity

Praised are you, Lord our God, king of the universe.
You created all things; therefore, all things are yours.
Wealth and honor come from you alone, for you rule over everything.
Power and might are in your hands,
and at your discretion, people are made great and given strength.
Oh our God, we thank you and praise your glorious name!
We are yours, and we adore you as the one who is over all things.
Oh Lord, you created us and, by your grace, redeemed and sustained us.
By your generosity, you gave us your Son, Jesus.
For we know the grace of our Lord Jesus Christ, that though he was rich,
for our sake, he became poor
so that through his poverty, we might become rich.
May the love of Christ compel us to no longer live for ourselves
but for him who died for us and was raised again.
As new creations, help us to walk in your ways
and repent daily of the things that hinder us.
Lord, we confess that our hearts are prone to wander,
making idols of our wealth and possessions.
We confess that we sometimes find our significance, security, and satisfaction
in our wealth and possessions.
We confess our tendency to store up treasure on earth rather than in heaven.
So, Lord, please open our eyes and hearts to see all that we have in Christ,
thereby freeing us from the deceptions caused by

the love of money and the illusion of control.
Help us to set our hope fully on you, Lord,
because in you, we have all that we need
for our enjoyment in this life and the age to come.
Help us to do good, be rich in good deeds,
and always be willing to share with those in need
so that we may store up treasures in heaven
and take hold of that which is truly life.
We offer this prayer in the name of the Father, the Son, and the Holy Spirit.[3]

3 This resource was developed in collaboration with Rick Steinberger, Michael Aitchison, Kent Sterchi, and David McKinney at the National Christian Foundation Orlando. For more information, visit https://www.ncfgiving.com/orlando/.

PART 1

Generosity Principles

What is a generosity principle? A principle is a timeless truth based on God's Word. More specifically, generosity principles are rooted in the teachings of Jesus Christ, who emphasized the importance of giving to others freely and generously. At its core, a generosity principle embodies the idea of selfless giving motivated by love and compassion rather than seeking recognition or reward. It reflects God's own generosity toward humanity, as demonstrated through his gift of salvation and abundant blessings. Generosity principles are the foundation from which we aspire to live out generosity practices.

The first four chapters of this book will discuss the generosity principles of experiencing God's generous love, being a faithful manager, being a generous sower, and living beyond blessed.

CHAPTER 1

God's Generous Love

Our inclination is to show our Lord only what we feel comfortable with. But the more we dare to reveal our whole trembling self to him, the more we will be able to sense that his love, which is perfect love, casts out all our fears.[4]

Henri Nouwen

Set your mind on things above, not on earthly things. For you died, and your life is now hidden with Christ in God. When Christ, who is your life, appears, then you also will appear with him in glory.

Colossians 3:2–4 NIV

Pursued by Love

Love is rooted in the righteous source of God the Father, God the Son, and God the Spirit, who rest at the core of our community of love. The Father loved by sending his Son to earth to display divine love with his life and to give his life in love as payment for our sins. The Son showed love by forgiving sins, healing bodies, and teaching eternal truths. The Spirit expresses love in unifying Christ's followers, guiding God's children, and drawing sinners to his irresistible love. God initiates his love to the undeserving so they can generously love others.

C. S. Lewis described how God pursues us, his creation. God is the wooer, and we are the wooed: "Our highest activity must be response, not initiative. To experience the love of God in a true, and not an illusory form, is therefore to experience it as our surrender to His demand, our conformity to His desire."[5] We experience the love of God by surrendering to his initiative to love us.

My wife, Rita, reminds me how a woman desires her lover to pursue her. She wants to feel valued. She wants to feel loved. The heart of her lover's affection

4 Henri Nouwen, "God's Love Casts Out All Fears," Henri Nouwen Society, April 12, 2024, https://henrinouwen.org.

5 C. S. Lewis, *The Problem of Pain* (HarperOne, 2001), 44.

is focused on her heart, desiring his very best for his bride. In like manner, Jesus Christ is pursuing us, his bride, to fully experience being beloved.

We encounter this central truth encapsulated in 1 John 4:19: "We love Him because He first loved us" (NKJV). This verse is the essence of divine love, unraveling the reasons behind God's love for humanity and the purposeful ways in which he personally loves us.

At the core of understanding why God loves us lies the intrinsic nature of God himself. The Bible teaches that God is love (1 John 4:8). He is boundless, selfless, and his unconditional love surpasses human comprehension. God's love is not contingent on our worthiness or actions; it emanates from his very being. It is a love that predates our existence and is rooted in the eternal nature of the Lord. Scripture reveals that divine love is deeply relational. Our Creator fashioned us in his image in the beginning, signifying an intimate connection. This generous act of creation reflects a deliberate choice to bring forth human beings capable of receiving and reciprocating divine love. God's love is not arbitrary but purposeful, driven by a desire for communion with his creation, most of all with his creation in his image, which includes you, his beloved child.

Furthermore, the Lord's love is manifested in his redemptive plan for humanity. Despite the rebellion and sinfulness of humanity, God initiated a rescue mission for you. The Bible narrates the story of salvation through Jesus Christ, the embodiment of God's love. John 3:16 articulates this divine initiative: "God so loved the world that he gave his one and only Son, that whoever believes in him shall not perish but have eternal life" (NIV). The sacrificial death of Jesus on the cross exemplifies the extent to which God is willing to go to reconcile you to himself.

The manner in which God loves you is multifaceted. His love is steadfast and unchanging, as depicted in Jeremiah 31:3: "I have loved you with an everlasting love; I have drawn you with unfailing kindness" (NIV). Divine love is not swayed by external circumstances or shortcomings; it remains a constant anchor in your life. Moreover, God's love is transformative. It has the power to change hearts, renew minds, and break the chains of sin. God's love doesn't leave you unchanged; it works in you, molding you into the image of Christ. Generous, heavenly love is a mystery that human intellect cannot fathom, yet it compels you to respond with gratitude, worship, and love in return.

So always sing his praises as the lover of your body, soul, and spirit pursues you. "I will sing of your love and justice; to you, Lord, I will sing praise" (Psalm 101:1 NIV).

Prayer: *Heavenly Father, I praise you for pursuing me with your generous love through Christ's love and in Jesus' name. Amen.*

The Power of Generosity: Because God first generously loved you, you are able to generously love.

We Become What We Love

Since somewhere around age ten, I have remembered this scene of the sounds and smells of autumn: a family of squirrels scurrying over crunchy leaves on an unseen mission, suddenly leaping vertically, twirling their way up an oak tree in a game of follow-the-leader—only the brave of heart leaping from one flimsy limb to another. I loved the outdoors, especially the woods. Inhaling fresh air fueled my imagination with new ideas and allowed me to play out my childhood dreams of becoming a forest ranger. As a curious adult, I still love God's creation and spend time outside reflecting on what could be. Being in God's creation stirs my heart to worship and be like my Creator. And as I focus on loving God in worship and prayer, my heart sings in praise of his generous love.

Where I set my affections, my heart and mind gravitate, and in the process, I become what I love. As I grow in my love for Jesus, I grow in my love of what he loves—a generous life of love.

The Lord's generous love reminds me of loving moms and dads holding their newborns, who coo, smile, and lock eyes with the ones they feel secure with, cared for by, and loved by. Parental and grandparental love are magnets that draw in the moldable hearts of little ones, who want to be like the ones who provide a safe environment for them to be themselves. We pray these little ones will grow up and learn how to love and follow Jesus. Children become aware that acceptance and affirmation from people who pay attention to them begin to craft their character into who they later become. Out of their hearts of humility, children have access to a full measure of love and grace. Children grow to become like the ones who love them and the ones they love. In God's grand design, the tender, humble heart of a child is fertile ground to plant seeds of generous living.

When we look at the life of Jesus, we see that a generous life is linked to a humble life. As we grow to embrace the humility of Christ's descension from heaven to earth—*humbling himself*—we learn to love humbling ourselves for another's sake. When we apply the humility of Christ's teaching and show compassion to sinners, we learn to generously love and not judge those ensnared by sin. When we empathize with the humility of Christ's prayerful struggle in the garden of Gethsemane and his obedience to die on the cross for the human race, we learn to love submission to God's will over our will. When we celebrate the humility of Christ's ascension back to heaven to intercede on our behalf, we learn to love the privilege of lifting up prayers for hurting people.

With humble gratitude, we make Christ the object of our affections. We become who we love and who loves us most: Jesus, our loving Savior and Lord. Our earthly generosity reflects our heavenly affections and love for what God loves.

Prayer: *Heavenly Father, grow my love for you so I become more like you. In Jesus' name. Amen.*

The Power of Generosity: When we set our affections on Jesus Christ, our hearts and minds grow more like his generous life.

Generous Love, Generous Forgiveness

As a freshman in college, I attended church with my then-girlfriend, Rita, and her family. I did not grow up attending church, so the songs and religious rituals were all new to me. After about six months of listening to the good news of Jesus Christ, I heard the pastor explain how my heavenly Father loved me with a love that would accept me for who I was, with all my sins and shortcomings, and how the Lord's generous love would cover me in abundant forgiveness.

What really drew me closer to God was the image of a heavenly Father's love and acceptance. I did not have this experience with my earthly father since he left our family when I was five years old. So in this sacred moment, I was captivated by this profound discovery: My heavenly Father's love embraced all of me beyond what I could ever imagine. He created me to be his own. He valued me as his beloved son. God's generous love and forgiveness freed me to love and forgive generously.

Luke 7:47 says, "I tell you, her many sins have been forgiven—as her great love has shown. But whoever has been forgiven little loves little" (NIV). From the lips of Jesus, we learn that the breadth of our forgiveness reflects the depth of our love. A person who is forgiven much loves much. Outside God's good grace, we all have the same wall of sin between God and ourselves. Our sins separated us from God, but the cross of Christ tore down sin's barrier. By faith, we are forgiven of our sins and adopted by God as his children. By receiving the grace of God, we transition from the rags of this world to the riches of heaven.

Forgiveness is cause for generous gratitude and thanksgiving. For some, forgiveness was more pronounced because sin was more prevalent. But upon further reflection, all of us must admit that our sin debt was more serious than we realized or were willing to admit. The lust in our hearts was controlling, and anger in our attitude was caustic. But God forgave us, and he still forgives us. This is another reason for love to resonate in our hearts. Not only has Christ forgiven us of past sins, but his grace also cancels out present and future debts of sin. God's love and forgiveness are generous.

There is no place you can go where the love of God cannot find you. You can run, but you cannot hide from the love and grace of God. If you are depressed, he loves and forgives you. If you are frustrated, he loves and forgives you. If you are confused, he loves and forgives you. If you are lost, he loves and forgives you. If you are afraid, he loves and forgives you. If you failed, he loves and forgives you. If you are unfaithful, he loves and forgives you. Nothing can separate you from the love and forgiveness of God.

You can love much because you have been forgiven much. Gratitude should explode from your heart when you ponder the depth of his forgiveness, the all-inclusiveness of past, present, and future sins wiped clean. God's grace generously removes your guilt and erases your shame. Your conscience is cleared. You are freed from sin to generously love. Your gratitude toward God will compel you to love him and love people. Sin has been replaced with your Savior, Jesus. He loves through your life. Love is your primary language because you are a beloved child of God—a new creation in Christ.

Christianity was not added to your life like a second bathroom added during a home renovation. Instead, Christ has become your life. Now, you live from the inside out. Jesus is doing a work in you to live his life through you. Your heart is full of love and forgiveness because of what God has done for you. You love continually and passionately because he has loved you with everlasting love. Meditate on and measure the extent of your forgiveness from God. Can you fathom where you would be without the grace and forgiveness of God? Celebrate his forgiveness with generous love.

Thank him often for his forgiveness. Show your appreciation to God for his forgiveness by loving others unconditionally. Love the undeserving. He did love. He does love. He will always generously love those undeserving of love. The forgiveness of God is matchless. The forgiveness of God is boundless. The forgiveness of God is freeing. The forgiveness of God facilitates love. The forgiveness of God produces generous love.

Let this truth consume and compel you: To be forgiven is to love. You can love much because you have been forgiven much. Because of the Lord's generous forgiveness toward you, your innermost self deeply desires to forgive others in a like manner—generously.

As the Lord clearly commands, "Be kind to one another, tenderhearted, forgiving one another, as God in Christ forgave you" (Ephesians 4:32 ESV).

Prayer: *Lord, thank you for forgiving me so freely. Help me reflect your grace by forgiving others with the same generosity. Let my heart mirror the mercy you've shown me. In Jesus' name. Amen.*

The Power of Generosity: A life that is generously forgiven is a life that generously forgives.

Fully Known and Loved

Jesus not only gave Mary Magdalene the generous gift of being known, but he also gave her the reassurance of making himself known to her. When Mary, out of love for her Lord, came to Jesus' tomb before sunrise, she was unable to find his body. Two angels sought to comfort her, asking, "Woman, why are you weeping?" (John 20:13 NKJV).

Before she had time to answer, a man whom Mary thought was the gardener approached her. He asked her the same question as the angels had asked and added another: "Whom are you seeking?" (v. 13).

Then, "Jesus said to her, 'Mary!' She turned and said to Him, 'Rabboni!' (which is to say, Teacher)" (v. 16). Jesus tenderly spoke her name, "Mary." When Jesus spoke her name, she turned to him, gazing into those loving eyes, and exclaimed back, "Teacher." Perhaps she remembered Jesus' prior teaching of his resurrection and now realized it had come to pass. In the process of being known by Jesus, she was able to know her risen Lord.

I remember, as a child, being reassured that my mom really knew me and loved me. Some days when I frustrated her, she might have mixed up my name with one of my other two brothers, Mitch and Jimmy. But I knew she was my biggest fan and would, to the best of her ability, care for me. Because of her consistent love, I trusted her and never doubted whether we would have enough for our family. She provided a hot meal each night for dinner and a warm home. Mom reflected for me my heavenly Father's tender love and concern. I could trust in his generous provision and care.

Isn't it so affirming when someone looks you in the eyes with a kind face and says your name? Maybe it means more to me since I have a unique Southern name. It's not unusual for me to be called Lloyd, Floyd, or Boy (reminds me of the young man in *The Jungle Book*, ha!). We once had a neighbor years ago whom I must have reminded of someone named Wade because that was the name I learned to respond to after several attempts to correct him.

Your name is the starting point of feeling known and loved. When another sees you only as a means to an end and as a transaction or, at worst, completely ignores you, insecurities, fear, and distrust can cripple the relationship. When someone understands you and cares for you, you cherish the safe place of being known. Everyone needs a safe place of generous love to process pain and grief.

All people have a tear in their hearts. A person in denial or with a hardened heart may argue against any apparent sadness in their life, but the reality is that we live in a broken, fallen world, and the shrapnel of sin has wounded every human being. Pain is a reality we all experience until, by God's grace and through faith in Jesus, we graduate to our heavenly home.

You may have been hurt by someone who is hurting. Instead of requiring a response that meets your standard for forgiveness, consider getting to know the other hurting soul. Your vulnerability to make yourself known can create a safe place for other weary ones to exhale and share their fears and insecurities. Learn a person's name and then ask the Holy Spirit to lead you in how to learn about the person behind the name. Do they have emotionally healthy or unhealthy parents? Are they experiencing physical challenges, emotional pain, or relational wounds?

And, of course, discover and affirm with others the moments they are most proud of and celebrate. Make a big deal of rejoicing over what other people make a big deal about.

But most of all, aspire to know and be known by the Father, Son, and Spirit. Lean into your heavenly Father's love and wisdom, learn from Jesus a gentle and meek spirit, and look to the Holy Spirit as your guide and comforter.

This is what Mary Magdalene did, as we can see in the post-resurrection exchange between Jesus and Mary. Henri Nouwen captured the essence of Jesus and Mary engaging on the high level of knowing and being known: "Mary feels at once fully known and fully loved. The division between what she feels safe to show and what she does not dare to reveal no longer exists. She is fully seen and she knows that the eyes that see her are the eyes of forgiveness, mercy, love, and unconditional acceptance.... What a joy to be fully known and fully loved at the same time! It is the joy of belonging through Jesus to God and being fully safe and fully free."[6]

As Nouwen said, what a joy to be fully known and fully loved at the same time! The more you grow in your understanding of being generously known and loved by the Lord, the more secure you will be in his care and provision and the more you will want what he wants for your life—a life that automatically reaches out to those around you with an attractive, generous love that makes everyone feel fully known and fully loved.

> O Lord, You have searched me and known me.
> You know my sitting down and my rising up;
> You understand my thought afar off.
> You comprehend my path and my lying down,
> and are acquainted with all my ways. (Psalm 139:1–3 NKJV)

Prayer: *Heavenly Father, thank you for knowing my name and for loving me and making yourself known through your Son, Jesus, through Christ's love, and in Jesus' name. Amen.*

The Power of Generosity: Generosity germinates in a heart that feels fully known and loved by God.

An Example of Intentional Love

Some very special women are worth emulating because of their Christlike ability to love unconditionally and with intentionality. My mother-in-law was a woman like that. Because of her lavish love toward me, I love her so much, and I deeply desire to love in the same manner as she did: freely, fully, and without reservations. Her generous love informs and inspires my generous love. In honor of my mother-in-law, Jean Isbill, who graduated to be with Jesus in 2020, here are ways she influenced me to be intentional with my bighearted love.

I learned from sweet Jean that intentional love requires prayerful awareness of those around me. It requires the Spirit's strength to see beyond me to what another needs and, by God's grace, to have a generous disposition that refuses to look down on others but looks up to the Lord for wisdom in how to love well. As Jesus said, "'Love your neighbor as yourself' [that is, unselfishly seek the best or higher good for others]" (Matthew 19:19 AMP). I want my love to be healthy,

---

6 Henri Nouwen, "The Joy of Belonging," Henri Nouwen Society, October 6, 2023, https://henrinouwen.org. Ellipsis in original.

looking first at how I am loved by my heavenly Father so that, in turn, I can love myself well, with a heart to love others in the same manner.

Gratefully, as I ponder Jean's and my Savior's love for me, I am reminded that he loves me with generous forgiveness, tender kindness, and nourishing care. Because my grateful heart is empowered with the Holy Spirit's energy and motivation, I can love in ways that help others notice God's love.

It makes me smile to reflect on three practical ways Jean loved me:

1. **Encouragement:** Jean affirmed my strengths, whether in my career, in my role as a husband, or in my parenting. Her praise bolstered my confidence because it demonstrated how much she appreciated me. She would say, "Boyd, God is using you to love your family well." Wow, did I ever need those words!
2. **Respect:** Jean honored the unique relationship I have with her daughter. She trusted us and allowed us the freedom to create our own family traditions. Respecting our boundaries and decisions strengthened our mutual understanding and love.
3. **Prayer:** I always knew Jean was lifting up my needs and asking God to bless and guide me with his wisdom. She genuinely cared for me and offered spiritual support. She would occasionally remind me that I was in her prayers, which warmed my heart.

Jean fostered a loving, respectful relationship with me through her encouragement, respect, and prayer. Her abundant love is a good transition for us to dive into the power of generous love.

Prayer: *Dear lover of my soul, thank you for your precious saints who show me how to love well. May my generous love be intentional so relationships in my life flourish for you. In Jesus' name. Amen.*

The Power of Generosity: A generous life that finishes well is a legacy that inspires and informs family and friends to live generously.

The Power of Generous Love

Even at our worst, the Lord has given us his best. So we start by being kind to ourselves. Our capacity to love is limited only by our kindness to ourselves. Then we can take the opportunity to be kind to those who are in trouble. We don't give up on those who despair because God, in his loving-kindness, has not given up on them. Job 6:14 tells us, "A person's friends should be kind to him when he is in trouble, even if he stops fearing the Almighty" (NCV). When we experience a spiritually dry season, we thirst for a cup of refreshing kindness, not dehydrating condemnation. Insults do not influence; they only alienate.

A soul distant from Jesus does not need a lecture on how far away they are from God; rather, they need to be reminded how close they are to "God's kindness," which "is meant to lead you to repentance" (Romans 2:4 ESV) and restoration. A dilapidated life can be rebuilt with one nail of kindness at a time: a kind smile, a kind word, a kind invitation for fun, or a kind gift. Love moves toward those tangled in trouble—not to fix their flaws but to show them in kindness that they are loved and not alone.

This verse exemplifies nourishing love: "No one ever hates his own body, but feeds and takes care of it. And that is what Christ does for the church" (Ephesians 5:29 NCV).

Just as you feed and care for your body, so you nourish your emotions with the goal of growing healthy relationships over time. To invest the time and training into emotional fitness is an expression of generous love. You nourish emotional health to understand better how to love those you value the most, who are precious to Jesus. Emotional neglect, evidenced by surface conversations, only ignores the realities of how the Lord has made us feel loved in our hearts. Just as a body is more susceptible to disease without proper care and feeding, so relational health deteriorates without the nourishment of generous love. Take the time to be with those who need you the most and make them feel known. The Holy Spirit bears beautiful fruit when we invest daily deposits of love relationally. Generous love nourishes relationships.

Prayer: *Heavenly Father, help me nourish others with the love and kindness you have generously given me. In Jesus' name. Amen.*

The Power of Generosity: God's generous love empowers us to bless those around us.

Wait on and Anticipate Generous Love

Maybe like you, I was spellbound by the opening scene of season one, episode one of *The Chosen*. Mary Magdalene was bound by seven demons who were battling for her soul. Then Jesus appeared to her with unconditional acceptance and generous love, moving her from bondage to evil and lies to freedom in his love and truth. And viewers watch her remain by Jesus' side throughout his ministry in an extravagant love and loyalty to her Master, Savior, and Lord. I mentioned Mary at the beginning of this chapter, explaining how we are shaped by what we love, and it is fitting to end this chapter with Mary's generous love.

"It was early on Sunday morning when Jesus came back to life, and the first person who saw him was Mary Magdalene—the woman from whom he had cast out seven demons. She found the disciples wet-eyed with grief and exclaimed that she had seen Jesus, and he was alive! But they didn't believe her!" (Mark 16:9–11 TLB).

The disciples had run away in fear for their lives, but Mary Magdalene had already surrendered her life to Christ with immovable, loving devotion. She was transformed by the Lord's love, which cast out her fears and seven demons. Mary Magdalene totally trusted that Jesus would do what he promised: rise again after three days. She was reassured since she had experienced Jesus bringing her back to life from being dead in her sins. Once controlled by demons of fear and shame, she was now set free by divine love and forgiveness. Mary couldn't be moved because forgiveness moved her to love much.

Charles Spurgeon, a brilliant English pastor of the nineteenth century, accurately and passionately celebrated Mary Magdalene's generous love for Jesus:

> Mary's heart was set on one object. Like an arrow shot from the bow, she sped right on to the target of her heart's desire. And, oh, if Christ be your one and only love, if your heart has cast out all rivals, if your spirit seeketh him, and crieth out for the Lord, even for the living God, you shall soon come and appear before God....
>
> ...What love was this! Brethren and sisters, if we would see Jesus, we must love him much. I would God I loved him as my heart desires to love him. I hope you can say, "Yes, I love thee, and adore; Oh for grace to love thee more!"[7]

Fear runs and exaggerates while love waits and anticipates. Fear says you are a failure. Love says that since you have remained faithful, you are successful. Fear rejects; love accepts. Fear says you don't matter. Love says you are precious and beloved. Fear obsesses over *what-ifs*. Love is hopeful over *what can be*.

Fear strives, and love abides. Abide in love, and fear will move away from influencing you. Fear is unwelcome and uncomfortable in the presence of Jesus Christ's generous love. Others you know may drift away from God and maybe

---

7 Charles Haddon Spurgeon, "Jesus Appearing to Mary Magdalene," The Spurgeon Center for Biblical Preaching at Midwestern Seminary, sermon given April 16, 1865, https://www.spurgeon.org.

even bolt away in unbelief; if so, remain anchored in love, and one day, those who went away may return longing for true love.

A Holy Spirit–heightened awareness of how the Father, Son, and Spirit have loved you, are loving you, and will love you is a guaranteed state of mind and heart to grow your generous heart of love. Like Mary, abide in Jesus, and the demons of fear will flee. And, like her, you may be in the presence of someone whom you think is a gardener, but in reality, you are in the presence of your loving Lord Jesus.

Keep pursuing Christ, especially when your spiritual vision is clouded. His love will reveal himself to you. The Spirit speaks through others, especially when you are having trouble seeing God at work in your life. Look for Jesus even among the dead since his heart is to bring the spiritually and physically dead back to life. Love waits and anticipates God's love. "To be loved by God is the highest relationship, the highest achievement, and the highest position in life."[8]

Prayer: *Heavenly Father, help me stand firm and immovable in your love for me and my love for you, anticipating by faith that your best is yet to be. Through Christ's love and in Jesus' name. Amen.*

The Power of Generosity: The more your love for the Lord grows, the more your heart yearns for generous time to be with Jesus.

Loved to Love Generously

Jesus Christ, on the night before the hardest day of his life, when he faced death, gave his disciples the gift of love. "A new command I give you: Love one another. As I have loved you, so you must love one another. By this everyone will know that you are my disciples, if you love one another" (John 13:34–35 NIV). Divine love is far superior to human love. The Lord's love is perfect; human love is imperfect. Christ's love is unconditional; human love is conditional. The love of God is limitless; the love of humans is limited. Divine love is diverse; human love is one-dimensional. Think of an earthly father whose love is admirable, but still, our heavenly Father's love far exceeds a loving dad's worthy example. Our Lord lavishes his love on our lives so we can lavishly love other lives.

We are loved by the Lord to love for the Lord. Christ calls us to love with a love not of this world. It is a love that can only be explained by an encounter with Almighty God. His transforming power on a humble heart positions his disciples to love on his behalf. Our Savior's parting words defined a radical love

8 Henry T. Blackaby and Claude V. King, *Experiencing God: Knowing and Doing the Will of God* (B&H Publishing Group, 2004), 84.

language, introducing the new nomenclature of how his disciples were to love. His command and promise to faithfully live make our generous living attractive to others, yet we rely on the Lord first loving us, as John reminded us: "We know and rely on the love God has for us. God is love. Whoever lives in love lives in God, and God in them" (1 John 4:16 NIV).

Our sequence of service and love starts with our brothers and sisters in the faith. If we ignore or harm our wounded, we are unattractive to an unloved world that experiences the same. Those who already live a low standard of love have little interest in exchanging it for another low standard. However, when we esteem the Lord's unconditional love for one another, we are attractive to the unsaved. For example, when fellow believers are caught in sin, they need our loving restoration, not harsh condemnation (Galatians 6:1–2). Generous love shows grace.

Our love for the Lord is evident when we do what we know to be true. Obedience to our loving, heavenly Father draws other potential disciples into our Father's forgiving arms of grace. We honor God when we show love for another child of God. Like siblings whose love for each other grows as they honor their parents, Christians who honor their heavenly Father grow in their love for one another. When we face our hardest days, we have an opportunity to extend generous love to those around us like Jesus did. Yes, as we are generously loved, we become Christ's channel to generously love like him.

"Dear friends, since God so loved us, we also ought to love one another. No one has ever seen God; but if we love one another, God lives in us and his love is made complete in us" (1 John 4:11–12 NIV).

Prayer: *Heavenly Father, help me abide in your love for me so I am able to love others like you love me. Show me who needs me to unconditionally love them today with your love in my heart. In Jesus' name. Amen.*

The Power of Generosity: Generously loving others flows out of being generously loved by Jesus.

Summary of "God's Generous Love"

- Because God first generously loved you, you are able to generously love.
- When we set our affections on Jesus Christ, our hearts and minds grow more like his generous life.

- A life that is generously forgiven is a life that generously forgives.
- Generosity germinates in a heart that feels fully known and loved by God.
- A generous life that finishes well is a legacy that inspires and informs family and friends to live generously.
- God's generous love empowers us to bless those around us.
- The more your love for the Lord grows, the more your heart yearns for generous time to be with Jesus.
- Generously loving others flows out of being generously loved by Jesus.

A Generous Prayer

Heavenly Father, I come before you in awe of your generous love, which knows no bounds. Your grace showers upon me endlessly, filling my life with blessings beyond measure. Thank you for the gift of your Son, Jesus Christ, who embodied your unfailing love through his sacrifice on the cross. Show me how you love me and what you have for me. May I be ever mindful of your abundant grace and mercy, which guide me in times of need and rejoice with me in times of joy. Show me how you would like for me to share your generous love with others, reflecting your kindness and compassion to all I encounter. In Jesus' name. Amen.

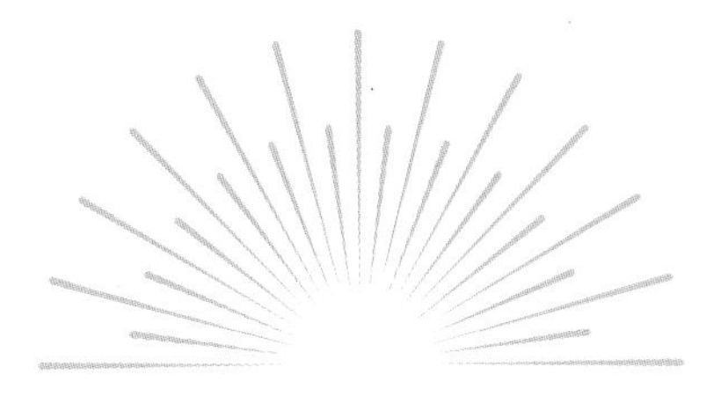

CHAPTER 2

Faithful Manager

God prospers me not to raise my standard of living,
but to raise my standard of giving.[9]

Randy Alcorn

It is required that managers be found faithful.

1 Corinthians 4:2 CSB

Who Owns What?

Tim Keller, the beloved now-deceased pastor, described how our view of ownership affects our generosity: "A lack of generosity refuses to acknowledge that your assets are not really yours, but God's."[10] Tim's keen insight illustrates how I lived for many years. I said God owned all I had but acted like I was in control of my stuff. Then God's Word and a charitable community called me out, urging me to experience the power of generosity through generous living.

I mentioned in the prologue that my wife, Rita, and I attended a small group Bible study on money early in our marriage. It was truly life-changing for both of us. Since I am a spender and she is a saver, we began to learn how our differences were actually very good for our marriage. I needed her to keep us disciplined within a spending plan—that is, a budget—as I was the visionary, always looking for wise ways to spend, invest, and give. God became our money mediator.

The first big idea we embraced together in our Bible study was that *God* is the owner of all we have. "Everything in the heavens and on earth is yours, O Lord" (1 Chronicles 29:11 NLT). We are called to be his faithful managers. Another way to describe our role as faithful managers is that our responsibility is to be fiduciaries of the Lord's possessions. What is a fiduciary? According to

9 Randy Alcorn, *The Treasure Principle: Discovering the Secret of Joyful Giving* (Multnomah Books, 2001), 75.

10 Timothy Keller, *Generous Justice: How God's Grace Makes Us Just* (Dutton, 2010), 91.

the US Consumer Financial Protection Bureau, a *fiduciary* is "someone who manages money or property for someone else. When you're named a fiduciary and accept the role, you must—by law—manage the person's money and property for their benefit, not yours."[11]

Instead of me trying to squeeze out another dollar for one of my ideas or Rita feeling bad for telling me no, we came up with a prayer for us to regularly ask our heavenly Father about his heart for our giving, saving, and spending: *Heavenly Father, how would you like for us to manage your resources? What is your heart for how you want us to invest in your kingdom? Our home, cars, bank account, and children are all yours. Show us your hilarious heart of generosity so that, in joyful gratitude, we may celebrate with generosity how you have abundantly blessed us.*

This shift in our mindset helped us to remember that all we have is the Lord's and that he has entrusted us with the responsibility to be generous overseers. We began to incorporate generosity into our everyday interactions. So for example, when one of our children misbehaved, we would silently pray, *Lord, give us generous love to discipline your child and ours.* When our car unexpectedly needed maintenance, we asked, *Lord, how would you like us to repair your car or maybe replace it?* Or when we faced a big, looming life decision, we confidently prayed, *All-knowing God, we need your wisdom. Help us remember that you give generously to all who ask.*

Prayers seeking God's heart for his resources grew us into more generous givers. But we still experienced tension in defining God's part to provide and our responsibility for planning ahead and working hard with wisdom. So we began to learn how the Holy Spirit brings clarity through prayer: *Lord, how much is enough?* Or we prayed the wisdom prayer in Proverbs 30:7–9:

> Give me neither poverty nor riches!
> Give me just enough to satisfy my needs.
> For if I grow rich, I may deny you and say, "Who is the LORD?"
> And if I am too poor, I may steal and thus insult God's holy name. (NLT)

And we experienced together how the Lord generously gives wisdom when we ask with a humble heart, as James 1:5 reminds us: "If you need wisdom, ask our generous God, and he will give it to you" (NLT). Prayer is how you express your dependence on the Lord.

11 "What Is a Fiduciary?" Consumer Financial Protection Bureau, last modified June 27, 2023, https://www.consumerfinance.gov.

Prayer: *Lord, I acknowledge that all I have is yours. Teach me to hold my blessings with open hands, sharing generously and using them for your purposes. Let my giving honor you. In Jesus' name. Amen.*

The Power of Generosity: Because God owns all I have, I will give my all to prayerfully oversee his generous blessings.

An Ongoing Tension

How much is enough? Over the years, I struggled with this elusive equation, so much so that I discovered, with the Lord's help, that I needed another more helpful question. *Is God big enough to provide for what's enough for me?* And like many questions for those of us who desire to fully follow Jesus and his plan for our lives, the answer to the rhetorical question is *Yes, yes, of course, the creator of the universe is large and in charge!* My needs are a penny of provision in God's economy. My Creator is certainly big enough to provide enough for me and my family. Since this is for sure, why do I still waver and, at times, doubt my heavenly Father's intentions and capacity to care for my needs beyond what I can ask or think?

Part of the tension is my lifelong struggle to discern what I am supposed to do and trust God for what he will do. In God's equation, being a responsible adult means to plan and provide and not strive. It also means I must trust in the Holy Spirit to lead me through the divine plan, seeking God's kingdom first and knowing all other necessities in life will follow. As Jesus says, since he cares for the birds and flowers, he will surely care for me and my family (Luke 12:24–28). Yet, growing up in a single-parent home, I became self-reliant at the early age of ten and learned to work hard and benefit from the fruits of diligent labor. Of course, as I later learned, there is nothing wrong with working hard as long as my work is unto the Lord (Colossians 3:23–24).

It seems that whatever season I find myself in, the lurking fear of not having enough is background noise to my responsible adult thinking. When we had small children, Rita and I worked hard to provide our four daughters with food, clothing, quality education, and nurturing in the ways of the Lord. As the girls grew into their teen years, we struggled to save and prepare for college and, eventually, four weddings. How would we pay for four weddings? Fortunately, God provided me with extra work to complement my minister's salary, and we lived on a strict budget.

To stay lighthearted, I did learn that the role of the father of the bride was to show up, shut up, and shell out! And stunningly, each wedding was less formal and more expensive. I never imagined the barns I stacked hay in as a young man could be such a significant revenue stream for aspiring entrepreneurs who lavishly repurposed the mundane for weddings. Barns are now used to host a catered barbecue and a band or DJ so guests can dance the night away with the smell of hay!

A responsible human desire is to have enough resources for life, especially for the expenses at the end of life. But how do we integrate having a plan with trusting God's plan? This helpful proverb comes to mind: "The heart of man plans his way, but the LORD establishes his steps" (Proverbs 16:9 ESV). We plan, and the Lord adjusts our choices and validates our way.

Now, in our empty-nest season, Rita and I still spend time discussing, planning, and being concerned about our future needs. Research tells us we are not alone, and one 2024 study showed that fears about the future are common:

- Nearly one in two older adults' biggest financial fear was not having enough money saved for retirement.
- One in four older adults fear they'll never pay off existing debt.
- Forty-five percent of people between ages fifty-five and sixty-four fear having high medical bills.[12]

These fears are only natural because our work lives have changed since the global pandemic in 2020. Millions of people lost their jobs, and many still have not returned to work. Some older adults may have had to leave work to become caregivers for their aging parents. This workforce migration we've recently seen has taken away many people's ability to earn money and save for their own retirement and future.

However, as followers of Jesus Christ, we have a higher call than just surviving or even thriving on earth. The sole focus of a committed Christ follower is to seek first the kingdom of God. In the process of seeking a purpose larger than life, our heavenly Caregiver cares for our life's needs. The shepherd of our souls is more than capable of being the shepherd of our stuff.

How much is enough? The Holy Spirit will lead his beloved ones to God's heart for us in answer to this question. Fear says there is never enough, but faith says the Lord's provision is enough. This doesn't mean we shouldn't plan well,

12 "Top 10 Fears of Older Adults in 2024," SeniorLiving.org, last modified April 12, 2024, https://www.seniorliving.org.

but it does mean that we should not obsess over stockpiling more than we need. Instead, we place our trust in our generous Lord—Jesus Christ.

In Luke 12, Jesus told the parable of the man who built a bigger barn to store his surplus. This story is packed full of emotion, wisdom, and warning. Jesus called out the prosperous man for his foolishness, shortsightedness, self-indulgence, and self-deception.

> God said to him, "You fool! This very night your life will be demanded from you. Then who will get what you have prepared for yourself?"
>
> This is how it will be with whoever stores up things for themselves but is not rich toward God. (vv. 20–21 NIV)

The productive man deceptively thought he owned his possessions: *his* crops, *his* barns, *his* grain, *him*self. The farmer even missed stating the obvious: Almighty God was the creator of the soil, his soul, and the harvest.

Our Creator generously cares for us, his creation, so our part in generous living becomes a lifelong discovery of how to be rich toward God. Jesus stated that the remedy for just building a life—a barn—for ourselves is to be rich toward God, but the foolish man failed to apply generosity as the antidote to greed and lived only for himself.

Rich Toward God

I continually have to ask myself if my life's motivation is to build my barns or if I am building God's barns by investing in the Lord's kingdom and not foolishly obsessing over my own kingdom. Before the barn story, Jesus dealt with two brothers who were bickering over their inheritance. The Lord used this conflict to illustrate a heart of greed. Wealth's seduction can simultaneously cause us to focus on the need for stuff while minimizing the need we feel for God. If I act like I am the owner of my possessions, then the acquisition of more possessions becomes my motivation. But if I live like the Lord is the owner of my stuff and I am his steward, then the distribution of his possessions becomes my passion. Generosity starves greed and casts out our fears. As followers of Jesus, if we focus on becoming more like generous Jesus, others will look to learn about following their generous Savior. Being rich toward God is valuing what God values over ourselves.

Here are some questions we can pray to learn how to be rich toward God:

- *Lord, how do you love and care for me, and how do you want me to love and care for others?*
- *Lord, how can I build the barns of your kingdom and avoid building bigger barns for myself?*
- *Lord, as my possessions increase, how can I increase my need for you?*
- *Lord, what is your heart for the possessions I manage for you?*
- *Lord, how can I be wise and not foolish in your eyes?*
- *Lord, are you enough?*
- *Lord, how can I be rich toward you?*

What does it mean to be rich toward God? It means to treasure what he treasures: our relationship with him, lost souls, love, and compassion for hurting human beings. To be rich toward God is to be rich in good deeds, generosity, and relationships. A few years after Christ's salient story of barn building and learning to be rich toward God, Paul challenged an emerging leader, Timothy, to command the rich in how to be rich toward God:

> Command those who are rich in this present world not to be arrogant nor to put their hope in wealth, which is so uncertain, but to put their hope in God, who richly provides us with everything for our enjoyment. Command them to do good, to be rich in good deeds, and to be generous and willing to share. In this way they will lay up treasure for themselves as a firm foundation for the coming age, so that they may take hold of the life that is truly life. (1 Timothy 6:17–19 NIV)

We are not meant to strive after wealth but to strive after God and share his blessings with others. This passage encourages us to view wealth as much more than security but as a tool to bless others. We can start by doing good wherever we can, actively looking for ways to serve and support those around us. This could be as simple as helping a neighbor or giving to a cause close to our heart. By choosing generosity, we're investing in something eternal beyond what money can buy.

Wealth can easily lead to arrogance or false security, but God calls us to humble dependence on him, knowing that he alone is the source of our blessings. When we're generous and willing to share, we experience "the life that is truly life"—a life of freedom, joy, and lasting purpose that reflects God's heart.

By doing so, we're laying up treasures in heaven and building a firm foundation for the future. We're embracing a life filled with purpose and aligned with the Lord's will. Today let's pray about how we can be generous and willing to share, trusting that our heavenly Father is our true provider.

Prayer: *Heavenly Father, inspire and instruct me to be rich toward you. In Jesus' name. Amen.*

The Power of Generosity: Being rich toward God is valuing what he values by doing good and being rich in good deeds with a willing, cheerful heart.

Faith's Abundance or Fear's Scarcity

Because of the relentless influence of fear, some followers of Jesus suffer from a scarcity mentality. A scarcity mentality is a belief that resources are always limited, so if someone has an abundance, there is less for you. American businessman and author Stephen Covey described the scarcity mentality this way: "People with a Scarcity Mentality have a very difficult time sharing recognition and credit, power or profit—even with those who help in the production. They also have a very hard time being genuinely happy for the successes of other people—even, and sometimes especially, members of their own family or close friends and associates. It's almost as if something is being taken from them when someone else receives special recognition or windfall gain or has remarkable success or achievement."[13]

Fear drives those who see the world as a place that lets them down by not providing the right amount of resources. A person with this limiting perspective is paralyzed from trying anything that seems out of the ordinary because of the fear of failure and the worry about losing what they have. The desire to hang on to people, things, and money captures the heart of someone who fears losing out. For the fearful, looking for ways to invest in people with time, money, or influence is not the best option. Not being generous (maybe even being greedy) is the safest way to live for the person who thinks of scarcity instead of abundance. Living with a defeatist scarcity mindset is emotionally exhausting, but being captivated by Christ's abundance energizes the soul and body.

Global activist and fundraiser Lynne Twist wrote about the lie of scarcity:

> We spend most of the hours and the days of our lives hearing, explaining, complaining, or worrying about what we don't have

13 Stephen R. Covey, *The 7 Habits of Highly Effective People: Powerful Lessons in Personal Change* (Free Press, 2004), 219.

> enough of....Before we even sit up in bed, before our feet touch the floor, we're already inadequate, already behind, already losing, already lacking something. And by the time we go to bed at night, our minds are racing with a litany of what we didn't get, or didn't get done, that day. We go to sleep burdened by those thoughts and wake up to that reverie of lack....
>
> This internal condition of scarcity, this mind-set of scarcity, lives at the very heart of our jealousies, our greed, our prejudice, and our arguments with life.[14]

Does this describe you? It can describe me at times. As the Lord leads me on this journey of generosity, he is teaching me to release my fears and focus on all he has blessed me with. An abundance mindset comes from trusting in heaven's limitless provision rather than focusing on what we lack. Jesus reminded us that our Father knows our needs and will provide (Matthew 6:31–33). Practically, this means resisting worry about resources and choosing to live generously. Instead of clinging tightly to our time, money, or talents, let's look for ways to bless others, confident that God replenishes what we give. We are blessed to begin each day by thanking God for his faithfulness, listing specific ways he has provided. As we rest in his love and trust in his abundance, we'll find freedom from fear and a greater joy in giving and sharing.

Instead of fearing scarcity, we should pursue what will last. "Do not store up for yourselves [material] treasures on earth, where moth and rust destroy, and where thieves break in and steal. But store up for yourselves treasures in heaven, where neither moth nor rust destroys, and where thieves do not break in and steal; for where your treasure is, there your heart [your wishes, your desires; that on which your life centers] will be also" (Matthew 6:19–21 AMP).

Prayer: *Lord, help me trust in your abundant provision. Free me from a scarcity mindset and let me live generously, knowing you supply all I need. My hope is in you alone. In Jesus' name. Amen.*

The Power of Generosity: Living with a defeatist scarcity mindset is emotionally exhausting, but being captivated by Christ's abundance energizes the soul and body.

14 Lynne Twist, *The Soul of Money: Transforming Your Relationship with Money and Life* (W. W. Norton, 2003), 44–45.

The Treasures of Jesus

What value do you assess to knowing the One and being known by the One? He knows you the best. Oh, the riches of his grace, the wealth of his wisdom, and the incalculable value of his vast love are reasons enough to shout hallelujah and praise him for his inexhaustible intimacy. You are a son or daughter of your great God and King. You were once alienated by sin's chaos but now are united to walk in calm trust with your heavenly Father, who prescribes your identity in Christ to secure your finite mind. Surrender to Jesus, bare your soul, and rest in his reassuring arms. Generosity grows when you know God and you are known by him.

We are created to spend more time with him—the one with whom we will spend all our time in eternity. Treasure Jesus by being with Jesus. Treasure Jesus by loving Jesus. Treasure Jesus by obeying Jesus. Treasure Jesus by learning of Jesus. Treasure Jesus by resting in Jesus. All other competing treasures can be left to rot in earth's trash heap when our heart is consumed by Christ alone. We treasure the Lord when we treasure what he treasures: worship, prayer, Scripture, and people.

May this be our heart's desire: "This, so that I may know him [experientially, becoming more thoroughly acquainted with him, understanding the remarkable wonders of his Person more completely] and [in that same way experience] the power of his resurrection [which overflows and is active in believers], and [that I may share] the fellowship of his sufferings, by being continually conformed [inwardly into his likeness even] to his death [dying as he did]" (Philippians 3:10 AMP).

Prayer: *Lord, give me a heart that treasures what you treasure. Help me value people, kindness, and eternal things above all. Make my heart generous, reflecting your love and priorities. In Jesus' name. Amen.*

The Power of Generosity: A heart that is generous toward God seeks to treasure what Jesus treasures: worship, prayer, Scripture, and people.

The Treasures of Relationships

Recently, I read a story of St. Laurence from early church history and was moved by Laurence's understanding of heavenly treasures:

> [He was] a 3rd century martyr killed during the persecution of Christians under Valerian. Laurence was a treasurer of sorts for the early Church, entrusted with the sacred vessels used in Christian

> worship. When the Romans got wind of this, they arrested Laurence and demanded that he bring the treasures to them. He agreed, and was given a few days to collect up the treasures and present them to the officials. When he returned, instead of offering golden vessels, he brought with him a group of people, each of whom were poor and needy. His response to the Roman guards? "Behold the treasures of the Church."[15]

St. Laurence's stunning demonstration of the true treasures of the church caused me to pause and ask myself, *What shiny, modern treasures vie for my affections? A new phone, a new outfit, a new car, a new video game, a new piece of jewelry, a new investment opportunity, or a new screen of some sort?* I possess a cornucopia of material treasure that competes with my modest heavenly treasures. Why? Because I am shortsighted and easily distracted by what makes me feel good at the moment. I become intoxicated by inferior treasures, even idols, and miss the true riches of sending treasures ahead for safekeeping with my Savior, Jesus. What are the best treasures I can send ahead and see again on display in God's kingdom? People are life's best investment.

What is a soul worth to our Savior? His life and death, for sure, and perhaps the cost of our life and death. Jesus loved people, forgave people, fed people, saved people, healed people, and comforted people. He was all about people! He built relationships with his disciples so they would love each other well and love others well. Friends and enemies felt Christ's love. Investing in relationships is a treasure that has a guaranteed kingdom return on investment.

How can we value relationships well? Investment of time, money, and emotional energy is a really good start. Understand another's needs and prayerfully connect them with the most appropriate resources. Sometimes the best approach in a relationship is a polite no or a thoughtful maybe based on your ability to serve well. Or you may be able to offer an energetic yes because you are totally at peace being a conduit for Christ. Relational growth happens intentionally and in life's messiness. As our generous love for people increases, it becomes evidence of our love for God. As the apostle Paul reminded the church at Thessalonica, "We ought always to thank God for you, brothers and sisters, and rightly so, because your faith is growing more and more, and the love all of you have for one another is increasing" (2 Thessalonians 1:3 NIV).

15 Tripp Prince, "What Do You Treasure?" Wisdom Hunters, August 26, 2021, https://www.wisdomhunters.com.

Prayer: *Lord, as I experience your love and grow in my love for you, let my heart overflow with love for others. Teach me to love generously in the same way you have loved me. In Jesus' name. Amen.*

The Power of Generosity: As God loves us and we love God, our love for people generously increases.

The Treasures of Giving Your Life Away

Our heavenly Father gave us his Son for salvation, and he gives us his Spirit for abundant living, so we gladly serve our radically generous God. He extravagantly gives us all we need to live well: salvation in Jesus that secures our eternal life with him, peace of mind knowing the Lord is in control, and serenity of heart knowing Christ is our calm in chaotic circumstances. God gives us management over his majestic creation and the wisdom to build and produce for the betterment of civilization. Generosity gushes from our heavenly Father like Lake Tahoe's pristine waters. As we swim in the Lord's generous waters, we are refreshed and refocused to live generously.

In what ways is Christ calling you to be generous? Certainly, your life can be a generous living sacrifice for the Lord. Each day you have the privilege to lay your agenda on the altar of obedience, allow the fire of the Holy Spirit to burn it up, and then grab God's game plan with the residue of righteousness. Daily you die to the need to *get* but come alive with the desire to *give*. Consider fostering or adopting a child, volunteering at church, serving in a public office, tutoring, or coaching. A variety of generosity is the best remedy for the various forms of greed Jesus warned us about: "Beware, and be on your guard against every form of greed; for not even when one is affluent does his life consist of his possessions" (Luke 12:15 NASB). A generous life is a happy life because when greed is at bay, generosity has its way. "We cared for you. Because we loved you so much, we were delighted to share with you not only the gospel of God but our lives as well" (1 Thessalonians 2:8 NIV). Where your treasure is, your heart will follow, so treasure the best treasures.

Prayer: *Heavenly Father, show me what you treasure so my heart may treasure the best treasures. In Jesus' name I pray. Amen.*

The Power of Generosity: A life given away to God is a life that gives away for God.

Treasure Hunting

I took a stroll one morning along a sandy, white beach on the Panhandle of Florida. My mission was treasure hunting for the grandkids. Shells, seahorses, and sand dollars all qualify as treasure for these bright-eyed, eager, and easily excitable grands. I was most intentionally looking for grayish sand dollars, which were somewhat hidden beneath the swirling, soft sand as the salty waves pulsated back and forth, exposing just enough for me to dig out a fully intact prize. The ultimate treasure was rare and beautiful, with imprinted lines and curves only God's imagination could create. I discovered that hunting for the most valuable treasure took time and persistence but paid off with great joy.

Jesus talked about hidden treasure: "The kingdom of heaven is like treasure hidden in a field. When a man found it, he hid it again, and then in his joy went and sold all he had and bought that field" (Matthew 13:44 NIV). The Master Teacher packed this one verse full of the memorable imagery of the kingdom of heaven as a hidden treasure. This most valuable discovery is for anyone who takes the time and effort to look for divine jewels, which are obtained by trust and maintained by obedience.

Jesus taught that the kingdom of heaven has come to earth and that all who submit to and follow King Jesus are servants in his kingdom. We need energy and intentionality to seek first the Lord's kingdom and trust that all other competing kingdoms will be subservient. God's kingdom currency is faith, love, and obedience. Joy results from treasuring what he treasures.

"From that time on Jesus began to preach, 'Repent, for the kingdom of heaven has come near'" (Matthew 4:17 NIV). When Jesus came to earth, he ushered in his kingdom for all who repent and believe in him. Responsible citizens of his kingdom are actively engaged in serving the poor and the rich. Have you submitted to the ruler of heaven and earth? Or do you carry a counterfeit passport that only represents your small, self-focused world?

Citizens of darkness delight in what delights the devil—being self-made instead of fearfully made—so stay in the light of God's kingdom, in a place of love and generosity toward people. Invest your life in the treasure of God's kingdom, and you will inherit life that is truly life. Wisdom pursues the Lord's kingdom now while anticipating being like him in the future. But to be passive, even to ignore the reigning King Jesus on earth, is to be massively deceived by the father of this world. Search and find the jewel of the Lord's love in an intimate relationship, labor in the fields of his kingdom, and celebrate his harvest of souls in praise and worship with "How Great Thou Art"—the King of kings and Lord of lords.

Treasure hunting for God brings joy and purpose to your life. "'Blessed is the coming kingdom of our father David!' 'Hosanna in the highest heaven!'" (Mark 11:10 NIV).

Prayer: *Heavenly Father, help me trust and obey as I seek first your kingdom through Christ's love and in Jesus' name. Amen.*

The Power of Generosity: Invest your life in the treasure of God's kingdom, and you will inherit life that is truly life.

Seek First God's Kingdom

I find myself excited about the possibilities of the near future and a little apprehensive about what might go wrong. In my tension, I have to remind myself that seeking God first does not eliminate uncertainty; in fact, walking with Jesus may invite uncomfortable, even painful, encounters over the next years. Yet my righteous God will do what's right and what's best for me. There's no need to fret about the future, but with eyes wide, I can gaze into the face of my faithful heavenly Father and receive his love and calming assurance. Spiritual stamina, financial provision, physical endurance, and relational health are God's generous gifts I can look forward to experiencing as we journey together.

Journeying with Jesus refuels my heart with his peace to live generously. Jesus himself encourages us to seek God's provision and blessings for the future by prioritizing our relationship with God and aligning ourselves with his purposes. We can eagerly anticipate his blessings and provision in the coming years, knowing he will abundantly provide for our needs. As we travel on our adventure of generous living, let us approach it with hearts overflowing with gratitude for God's faithfulness. Let us celebrate his past blessings, acknowledging his timely provision, guidance, and presence in our lives. Simultaneously, let us eagerly anticipate the unfolding of his plans, trusting in his promises and seeking his kingdom above all else.

As Matthew 6:33 says, "Seek first the kingdom of God and His righteousness, and all these things shall be added to you" (NKJV). What does it look like to seek the kingdom of God first? Nuance is necessary since subtle competitors bid us to seek them first in the name of seeking God's kingdom first. For example, money often tempts me to place my security and value in material wealth rather than in God's promises. It can subtly shift my focus from eternal priorities to temporary gains. Fortunately, the sweet Holy Spirit nudges my spirit to seek his kingdom first, reminding me that true fulfillment and security are found only in him, not in wealth.

A kingdom-first mindset is not easily distracted by positive or negative circumstances. A positive experience is how an answered prayer of healing may invigorate the faith of a faithful community, but healing should not become an end in itself. Instead, seeking God's kingdom is the ongoing focus. Good things become a distraction from God's best when we don't put first the greater purpose of seeking first the kingdom of God. Or when a tragedy, like the loss of life or health challenges, rocks the world of a family, friends, and a church community, comfort and grief are God's means of healing and recovery. Yet getting stuck in the loss instead of seeking first the Lord's kingdom only dilutes divine influence.

Sometimes I let particular people influence my thoughts and actions more than I should. Their opinions and desires can distract me from God's truth, diluting his voice in my heart. Wisdom reminds me to surround myself with those who encourage my faith and help me grow closer to Christ.

Life is a daily experience of joy and sorrow, so whatever the circumstances we find ourselves in, we must stay focused on the loving face of our heavenly Father and his kingdom vision. To love is to intentionally and generously seek first the kingdom of God.

As we reflect on a more intentional life of generosity, it is an opportune moment to recall the abundant blessings our gracious and faithful God has bestowed on us in the past. Amid life's joys, challenges, and uncertainties, Scripture reminds us to celebrate and acknowledge God's goodness while eagerly anticipating his blessings in his timing. Scripture resounds with exhortations to praise and offer thanksgiving for God's abundant blessings. Psalm 103:2 declares, "Bless the Lord, O my soul, and forget not all His benefits" (NKJV).

As we journey with Jesus, it's crucial to anticipate the future with hope and trust in God's providence. Jeremiah 29:11 assures us of God's plans for our future: "I know the plans I have for you, declares the Lord, plans for welfare and not for evil, to give you a future and a hope" (ESV).

God's faithfulness in the past serves as an anchor of assurance, reminding us that his plans for us are filled with hope and goodness. Walk with Jesus on this journey of generosity by seeking his kingdom with humility and wisdom. And like Solomon, you may be given more than you ever imagined: "I have also given you what you have not asked: both riches and honor, so that there shall not be anyone like you among the kings all your days" (1 Kings 3:13 NKJV). As C. S. Lewis accurately reminded us, "If I find in myself a desire which no experience in this world can satisfy, the most probable explanation is that I was made for another world."[16]

Prayer: *Heavenly Father, I look forward to journeying with you for the rest of my life. As I encounter ups and downs, I will seek your kingdom first through Christ's love and in Jesus' name. Amen.*

The Power of Generosity: A life of prayer and intentional generosity seeks first the kingdom of God.

A Modern-Day Parable of Kingdom Living

I read this clever story on a silent retreat, and it captured my heart and imagination to lean into living for the Lord's kingdom and not my own:

> Once upon a time, in a not-so-faraway land, there was a kingdom of acorns, nestled at the foot of a grand old oak tree. Since the citizens of this kingdom were modern, fully Westernized acorns, they went about their business with purposeful energy; and since they were midlife, baby-boomer acorns, they engaged in many self-help courses. There were seminars called "Getting All You Can out of Your Shell." There were woundedness and recovery groups for acorns who had been bruised in their original fall from the tree. There were spas for oiling and polishing those shells and various acornopathic therapies to enhance longevity and well-being.
>
> One day, in the midst of this kingdom, a knotty little stranger suddenly appeared, apparently dropped "out of the blue" by a passing bird. He was capless and dirty, making an immediate negative impression on his fellow acorns. Crouched beneath the oak tree, he stammered out a wild tale. Pointing upward at the tree, he said, "We…are…that!"
>
> Delusional thinking, obviously, the other acorns concluded, but one of them continued to engage him in conversation: "So tell us, how would we become that tree?" "Well," said he, pointing downward, "it has something to do with going into the ground…and cracking open

16 C. S. Lewis, *Mere Christianity* (HarperSanFrancisco, 2000), 136–37.

the shell." "Insane," they responded. "Totally morbid! Why, then we wouldn't be acorns anymore."[17]

This clever and convicting acorn story inspires an important application question: Which kingdom has your loyalty: your tiny acorn kingdom or God's massive kingdom of trees?

As Christians, we are called to be faithful managers of God's kingdom, using our resources, time, and gifts to serve him. This means aligning our choices with his values and prioritizing his purpose over personal gain. We seek to remain loyal by keeping our hearts focused on Christ, staying in his Word, and seeking his guidance daily. By honoring him in small and big decisions, we can reflect his love and build his kingdom faithfully in the Spirit's power.

Summary of "Faithful Manager"

- Because God owns all I have, I will give my all to prayerfully oversee his generous blessings.
- Being rich toward God is valuing what he values by doing good and being rich in good deeds with a willing, cheerful heart.
- Living with a defeatist scarcity mindset is emotionally exhausting, but being captivated by Christ's abundance energizes the soul and body.
- A heart that is generous toward God seeks to treasure what Jesus treasures: worship, prayer, Scripture, and people.
- As God loves us and we love God, our love for people generously increases.
- A life given away to God is a life that gives away for God.
- Invest your life in the treasure of God's kingdom, and you will inherit life that is truly life.
- A life of prayer and intentional generosity seeks first the kingdom of God.

17 Cynthia Bourgeault, *The Wisdom Way of Knowing: Reclaiming an Ancient Tradition to Awaken the Heart* (Wiley Publishers, 2003), 64–65. Ellipses in original.

A Generous Prayer

Heavenly Father, grant me the strength and wisdom to be a faithful manager of all you've entrusted to me. Help me steward my time, talents, and resources in accordance with your will, honoring you in all I do in your kingdom work. May my actions reflect your goodness and grace as I serve others with love and humility. Guide me to invest in eternal treasures and to seek your kingdom above all else. May I hear you say, "Well done, faithful servant," when I stand before you. Amen.

CHAPTER 3

Diligent Sower

The longer I live, the more I am enabled to realize that I have but one life to live on earth and that this one life is but a brief life, for sowing, in comparison with eternity, for reaping.

George Müller

He who supplies seed to the sower and bread for food will supply and multiply your seed for sowing and increase the harvest of your righteousness. You will be enriched in every way to be generous in every way, which through us will produce thanksgiving to God.

2 Corinthians 9:10–11 ESV

A Diligent Sower

Elver is my new hero. Somehow, he was able to transform our half acre of hard dirt, roots, weeds, vines, and buried brick into green fields that were only in my dreams. The fescue-seeded miracle is soft and durable enough for our grandkids to play sports and for Easter eggs to get lost in the hunt, buried in vibrant green blades of grass.

I watched Elvar's secret in amazement. First, he and his crew of four hard-working men totally cleared out the roots, weeds, rocks, and other obstacles to growing healthy grass. Then, they triple-aerated and generously seeded the revitalized dirt. From my novice view, it seemed like Elver overseeded. Not to mention, he worked in the heat of August, not the cooler days of October when most people seed grass. Well, I'm glad I was not in charge because over the next few months, God blessed us with rain while the grass grew in proportions that could have been baled if our lawn had been a hayfield.

Elver prepared the ground. God supplied the generous seed, rain, and the abundance of green grass. I learned that soil preparation, quality and quantity of seeds, and timely rain showers are a recipe for an abundance of fruit or, in this case, luscious green grass.

In God's fields of loving people and living generously, a diligent sower thoroughly prepares, generously gives, and trusts the Lord of the harvest for beautiful results.

Seeds of Love

Rita and I recently celebrated our friend Pam's life after she went to be with Jesus. For more than eighteen months, Pam battled ALS, a harsh disease that squeezed life from her body with daily doses of deterioration. Her husband, Randy, served her in love, strengthened by Holy Spirit resolve. Pam's friends showered her with 165 meals and 650 cards of encouragement. She reaped a harvest of love because, almost every day of her life, Pam planted seeds of love. A genuine smile. A listening ear. A comforting prayer. A timely gift. She was a generous lover.

Paul expanded on Jesus' parable of the sower by explaining the principle of sowing and reaping, which was most relevant in their agrarian society but still applicable in our modern times. "He who supplies seed to the sower and bread for food will supply and multiply your seed for sowing and increase the harvest of your righteousness. You will be enriched in every way to be generous in every way, which through us will produce thanksgiving to God" (2 Corinthians 9:10–11 ESV). Gardens grow when someone prepares the soil, plants good seeds, pulls the weeds, and waters the sprouts—all with daily nurturing. In time and under the right conditions, seeds sown reap a harvest. The same idea relates to seeds of love sown in the lives of others. Those who generously sow love in other people can expect to harvest generous love. Seeds of love grow to enrich you in every way to be generous in every way.

The eloquent prophet Isaiah captured the imagery of God's Spirit revitalizing the land and empowering lives in righteous living when he wrote, "So it will be until God pours out the Spirit from up above, and the land comes alive again—desert to fertile field, fertile field to forest. Then justice and truth will settle in the desert places, and righteousness will infuse the fertile land" (Isaiah 32:15–16 VOICE).

The Holy Spirit is the originator and initiator of love that lasts. The divine roots of love go deep into the soil of a humble heart, ever ready to serve another in Jesus' name. As you submit to the Spirit's influence, the fruit of the Spirit will be evident in your life, with "love, joy, peace, patience, kindness, goodness, faithfulness, gentleness, self-control" (Galatians 5:22–23 ESV). A Spirit-filled life is capable only of loving. Just as sunflower seeds grow brilliant yellow flowers, so the seeds of love grow an attractive, irresistible life. Generous living plants seeds of love in the power of the Spirit.

Are you a generous lover whose life and death will be defined by an abundant harvest of love? Every day, look for ways to plant the seeds of love. Look into the eyes of someone who serves you either personally or professionally, say their name, and thank them for their work. Slow down and get to know those around you—their dreams and desires, the names of their spouse and children. Learn the love language of family members, friends, and work colleagues so you can love them in a way that makes them feel loved. Sow seeds of love in Jesus' name, and an orchard of love will remain beyond your death. Like Pam's life demonstrated, a zeal for loving others will follow for generations to come.

Prayer: *Heavenly Father, each day by the power of your Spirit, lead me to plant seeds of love in other hearts through Christ's love and in Jesus' name. Amen.*

The Power of Generosity: Seeds of love grow to enrich you in every way to be generous in every way.

Cheerfully, Freely Given

After explaining the promise of sowing and reaping, Paul described the spirit and attitude we should have in our sowing and reaping: "The point is this: whoever sows sparingly will also reap sparingly, and whoever sows bountifully will also reap bountifully. Each one must give as he has decided in his heart, not reluctantly or under compulsion, for God loves a cheerful giver" (2 Corinthians 9:6–7 ESV). We are to give cheerfully, not under compulsion. The apostle beautifully described generous giving as a heartfelt experience led by the Holy Spirit. Giving is an act of worship humans offer to God, not a feeling of manipulation between people or organizations.

How we handle money reflects what our heart truly treasures: God or money. Like the love a grandparent feels after receiving a joyful grandchild's drawing of their hand outlined to look like a turkey, with coloring outside the lines, so the Lord loves to see his children give genuine, heartfelt gifts to those they care about. God's love follows happy givers.

Several years ago, my wife and I met a new friend at a Generous Giving Celebration event. Roger was reeling over a recent divorce and teetering on the edge of depression. The pain etched on his face made him look unhealthy and unpleasant. We listened a lot and attempted to comfort him with our limited capacity, but God showed up through the worship, teaching, and testimonies to grow Roger's heart with hope and wholeness, much like the growing of the Grinch's small, angry heart. The Lord convicted Roger to give his way out of his hurt.

Generosity is one of God's strategies for healing and happiness. Greed tends to measure success in life by how much we get, not by how much we give. Yet Jesus, like he did so many other times, reversed the order when he said, "Beware! Guard against every kind of greed. Life is not measured by how much you own" (Luke 12:15 NLT).

Winston Churchill, the famous British statesman, nailed this idea of giving over getting when he said, "We make a living by what we get, but we make a life by what we give."[18] If we give to get, disappointment will stalk us, and our reward becomes earthbound. When we give cheerfully, expecting nothing in return, fulfillment will invade us, and our rewards will extend eternally. Quietly ask your heart, *What is God's heart?* and then follow his heart. His heart is for the poor, so give to the poor. His heart is for the church, so give to the church. His heart is for missions, so give to missions. Generous living follows the Lord's heart.

When we view giving as worship, we are grateful and prayerful. We are grateful because of God's gift of life, his comfort in death, his support in suffering, his wisdom in decision-making, and his assurance of salvation in Jesus. We are prayerful because we desire to live according to God's will. Who needs our exuberant generosity? We do! Giving as worship draws us to God, who fills our hearts with love. When we get down, we must look up and ask the Lord where we can cheerfully give. Jesus' love is unleashed in the life of a joyful giver. Those who are generous feast on the fruit of joyfulness. "If [your gift] is to encourage, then give encouragement; if it is giving, then give generously; if it is to lead, do it diligently; if it is to show mercy, do it cheerfully" (Romans 12:8 NIV).

Prayer: *Heavenly Father, help me know your heart and be a cheerful giver. In Jesus' name. Amen.*

The Power of Generosity: When we get down, we must look up and ask the Lord where we can cheerfully give.

18 Winston Churchill, *Churchill by Himself: The Definitive Collection of Quotations* (Public Affairs, 2008), 576.

Uber Generous

Early one morning on the drive to the Hartsfield–Jackson Atlanta International Airport, my Uber driver, Ash, shared some of his life story. Growing up in another country, he has lived in America off and on over the past thirty years. Without me bringing up that I worked for the National Christian Foundation, he shared with me how he marveled at the generosity of Americans. Over three decades, he had observed how abundantly Americans love their families. This surprised him since he had been taught as a young man that Americans always worked and did not have time for family. But after moving to Atlanta in the 1990s, he was invited more than once into the homes of friends and was pleasantly surprised by the warm and loving families he visited. He experienced the generous hospitality of a family coming together to make him feel welcome.

I was so inspired to hear how generous hospitality had blessed my new friend. But there was more. Our drive was about fifty minutes, so he continued to share with me another generous activity of his. When tipped with cash, he places this unexpected financial blessing, what he calls "found money," in the middle console of his car. At certain stoplights in the city, he encounters those seeking generous givers, so he gives a couple of bucks to that person in need who may be standing outside his window.

Then, as I felt the energy in his voice rise, he joyfully declared, "Some passengers witness my small act of generosity and will contribute an additional ten dollars to my giving fund that I tuck into my cubbyhole between the seats." Ash was describing the scriptural principle of sowing and reaping.

Whenever we sow, we will reap. Our reaping may be monetary, but it could just as easily be a simple thank-you. And the results of our sowing may extend beyond the immediate. Yes, we may feel a momentary satisfaction of being the Spirit's vessel of blessing, but in relationships, reaping results takes time. For example, there may be a time lapse between sowing truth into a child's heart and reaping consistent character transformation. Just as seeds need to be planted and watered before they germinate, so a relationship takes years of sowing patient love to reap the fruit of trust and intimacy. Beautifully, my new friend, Ash, is uber-generous as an Uber driver!

The Power of Generosity: Spontaneous seed sowing reaps unexpected blessings to the giver and the receiver.

The Gift of a Life Prepared to Meet God

My friend Charlie Renfroe gave his family the gift of knowing he was a passionate follower of Jesus Christ. Not only as he approached the valley of the shadow of death but throughout his adult life, his wife and children knew he knew Jesus. Like Charlie, are you ready to meet God? Have you given your spouse and children the assurance that you have received by faith the indescribable gift of Jesus Christ as your Savior? The assurance of your spiritual preparation to meet God after death is a generous gift to your family and those who love you.

I was with Charlie and his wife, Patty, at their home to plan his funeral. The doctor said it could be two hours, two days, or two weeks before he breathed his last. Shock and awe filled us all as my mentor for thirty years faced his final few days before going to his eternal home with God. A blend of family and friends, about ten of us, gathered at my friend's home to sit together in what became a sacred moment as we wept, laughed, comforted, and celebrated a life lived with intentionality for the Lord's priorities: faith, family, generosity, and love. The fruit of Charlie's influence was in the room and beyond. A relational orchard, you could say. We were unable to recount or even comprehend all the seeds of influence his life had planted over the years.

When you cut open an apple, you can count the seeds, but when you plant a seed, you are unable to count how many apples it will produce. Charlie's life was a seed he planted in the Holy Spirit's power to grow an orchard for God. His life reminds me of these words of Jesus: "Truly, truly, I say to you, unless a grain of wheat falls into the earth and dies, it remains alone; but if it dies, it bears much fruit" (John 12:24 ESV). Charlie's life also reminds me of Paul, who prayed and wept with and comforted those who loved him right before he left on his last assignment for the Lord (Acts 20:34–38), which eventually led to imprisonment and death. Charlie comforted us with words of peace, blessing, and gratitude. We were there to comfort him, yet the Holy Spirit breathed life-giving words through his beloved son to bless us.

Another God moment in our sacred gathering occurred when the question arose about how we will look in heaven. What will our bodies be like? What age will we be? Thirty-three, the age of Jesus when he died? Will those who died as children be grown or still children in heaven? Our pastor, Andy, shared helpful words penned by Paul, who described our bodies as seeds:

> Someone may ask, "How will the dead be brought back to life again? What kind of bodies will they have?" What a foolish question! You

> will find the answer in your own garden! When you put a seed into the ground it doesn't grow into a plant unless it "dies" first. And when the green shoot comes up out of the seed, it is very different from the seed you first planted. For all you put into the ground is a dry little seed of wheat or whatever it is you are planting, then God gives it a beautiful new body—just the kind he wants it to have; a different kind of plant grows from each kind of seed. (1 Corinthians 15:35–38 TLB)

All seeds are unique. Some grow into trees, others flowers, some vegetables, and the list goes on. The varieties within each group are diverse. Yet all are seeds. And all have to be buried and die to come alive.

So with blurred eyes of faith, we can imagine our bodies as unique, shriveled seeds going back to the dust of the earth where we came from, only to come alive with God with beautiful, glorified bodies. You will be you—no one else like you—as your spirit within your earthly body will live on forever in your heavenly body. God's Word gives us a glimpse into our beautiful, wonderful bodies.

The body is sown perishable and is raised imperishable; sown in dishonor, raised in glory; sown in weakness, raised in power; sown natural, raised spiritual (1 Corinthians 15:42–44). The beauty and brightness of our heavenly bodies will be attractive to the eye and energizing to all. Like a caterpillar bursting forth from its chrysalis, so we will fly out of our graves to be with the Lord in beauty and splendor, clothed in the likeness of our Savior, Jesus Christ.

Will our bodies really be like Jesus'? Indeed, "Our citizenship is in heaven, and from it we await a Savior, the Lord Jesus Christ, who will transform our lowly body to be like his glorious body" (Philippians 3:20–21 ESV). Heaven will be shrouded in the splendor of your glorified body, and in the process, your Eternal Lover will transform you to be like him and to be with him, uniquely you, because there are no other human beings like you, from your fingerprints to your complex genetic design. Your earthly body must die to come alive by the transforming power and love of God.

As we finished up our sacred gathering with tears, hugs, and forced smiles, a tinge of jealousy stuck its head out of my heart, reminding me, *My good friend will soon be with our best friend.* I could celebrate an eighty-one-year life lived with love, generosity, and kingdom purpose, which was a life that was now dying the same way. Charlie was facing death as he had lived. Death is defeated; however, the true enemy is a life unprepared for death.

Will you prepare to meet your God with repentance and faith in Jesus? When you prepare to meet the Lord, you can know and be assured that "to be absent from the body" is "to be present with the Lord" (2 Corinthians 5:8 KJV).

Prayer: *Heavenly Father, thank you for your promises to give me a unique body in heaven that looks and acts like Jesus. Through Christ's love and in Jesus' name. Amen.*

The Power of Generosity: The assurance of your spiritual preparation to meet God after death is a generous gift to your family and those who love you.

Sow Generous Tears of Grief

Tears of grief transcend our everyday emotions, for they come from deep within our hearts and can erupt in uncontrollable sobbing. God gives us tears of grief to express our larger-than-life losses. In the Lord's mercy, he allows us to weep. Tears of grief can flush out our fears and foster our faith, representing a cleansing process. "Those who sow with tears will reap with songs of joy. Those who go out weeping, carrying seed to sow, will return with songs of joy, carrying sheaves with them" (Psalm 126:5–6 NIV). Tears stream down our faces and cloud our eyes, but we see Christ when they subside. We see him as our comfort and caregiver. We may have been caregivers, but now we need a caregiver.

In our loss, we need the Lord. We need the comfort of Christ to wipe away our tears and replace them with his hope. God shows up in our tears of grief through sympathy and soul care. Our tears of grief elicit our Savior's tender touch. What you have lost, you may not get back soon. It is gone, and its destiny is in God's hands, but do not lose hope. Heaven wants to help. God is not passively dispassionate about your despair; he cares.

Your loss may be that of loved ones who voluntarily disassociated from your family. Perhaps they grew tired of your influence and authority and wanted to see the world for themselves. Their departures may have been sudden and unexpected. You weep because you wonder if they will ever come back the same. Pray that Christ will change them on that journey to find themselves. Pray they find him and embrace the good values you have instilled in their character. God will use your tears to keep your loved one's heart tender for him. Present your tears of grief as a humble offering to him.

Your loss may be material. The perceived value of these personal treasures is contingent on your capacity to remember. Your photos may still be framed in your mind's eye though now absent from their frames. Thank God you can still remember since memories are his gifts to be cherished and celebrated. Do not allow the physical loss to rob you of its emotional significance. Moreover, do not focus on fleeting financial losses. Money-motivated living makes for a roller-coaster ride of uncertainty. Your grief will never subside if it depends on dollars.

Let the Lord and others love you through your grief. God grieves with you. He gave his Son, so he understands loss. Jesus weeps when you weep, so you are not alone in your pain and suffering. Tears are a liquid bridge to the Lord. They are a float of faith down the river of God's will. Grief is meant to lead you to the Lord. Therefore, receive the warm embrace of your heavenly Father and invite his children to pray and care for you. When your tears subside, stay at the side of your Savior, Jesus. Your weeping has washed your soul for service, and now you can tenderly engage with others in their tears.

Use grief to leverage your life for the Lord and for the grieving. You can be generous in your comfort for others in their grief since God and others have been generous in their comfort for you. The Bible says, "We can comfort those in any trouble with the comfort we ourselves receive from God" (2 Corinthians 1:4 NIV).

Prayer: *Heavenly Father, I receive your comfort as my heart weeps over a great loss. Fill the hole in my heart with your grace and love. In Jesus' name. Amen.*

The Power of Generosity: Sowing tears of grief brings comfort and healing to the heart.

A Life Built to Last

Truett Cathy, the admired founder of Chick-fil-A, wisely mused, "It is better to build boys than to mend men."[19] The idea is that it's better to take a preventative approach to building an intentional life rather than a presumptuous, passive approach that leaves us one day picking up the pieces from unwise choices. Sowing seeds of wise choices reaps a solid foundation for generous living. Jesus said, "Everyone who hears these words of mine and puts them into practice is like a wise man who built his house on the rock" (Matthew 7:24 NIV). Whether one is building a house, business, ministry, or life, they all require timeless principles: a proven plan, a supportive team, and practical application with a heart and mind of wisdom. A life that is able to withstand and even overcome life's trials is built on the foundation of faith in Jesus Christ. Christ, the Cornerstone, is an immovable and solid structure to support an abundant life.

19 S. Truett Cathy, *It's Better to Build Boys Than Mend Men* (Looking Glass Books, 2004).

Jesus, being a carpenter by trade, contrasted from experience a house with structural integrity with one foolishly constructed. He described in detail two types of life foundations: one built on the rock and one built on the sand. Those foundations reflect the solid rock of faith in Jesus Christ as your Savior or the shifting sand of self-reliance and self-righteousness. On the rock foundation, a wise builder uses bricks of obedience, not the straw and sticks of sinful living. So when the storms of life hit hard, a life built on belief in God is supported by a loving community that helps repair the damage. The ultimate storm is the final judgment, where the quality of each person's work is tested. The fire will burn away the wood, hay, and straw of sin, but the precious metals of obedience remain. "If anyone builds on this foundation using gold, silver, costly stones, wood, hay or straw, their work will be shown for what it is, because the Day will bring it to light. It will be revealed with fire, and the fire will test the quality of each person's work" (1 Corinthians 3:12–13 NIV).

To be a wise life builder is to be obedient to Christ's commands, and to be an unwise life builder is to be foolish and disobedient to Christ's commands. Have you placed your total trust in the rock of Jesus Christ? Once you have Christ as your chief cornerstone, you are able to build a life of love, brick by brick, with little acts of kindness, anonymous gifts of generosity, and seeds of hope that, over a lifetime, grow orchards of beautiful fruit in other lives.

Charles Spurgeon described the peace of mind and heart of the life that is well built on Christ: "The Christian rests peacefully upon Christ. Troubles come one after another, but they do not sweep him away, they only endear to him the hope which is based upon Christ Jesus. And when at last death comes, that awful flood which will undermine everything that can be removed, it cannot find anything to shake in the wise builder's hope. He rests on what Christ has done; death cannot affect that. He believes in a faithful God; and dying cannot affect that."[20]

Seek to build your life on Christ and help others to faithfully build on him. Then rest in his security. And when death knocks at the door of your life, you can rest in what comes next—Jesus Christ. Building on Christ's foundation is sowing seeds that will reap a life of faithfulness that finishes well. "He was looking forward to the city with foundations, whose architect and builder is God" (Hebrews 11:10 NIV).

20 Charles Haddon Spurgeon, "The Two Builders and Their Houses," The Spurgeon Center for Biblical Preaching at Midwestern Seminary, sermon given February 27, 1870, https://www.spurgeon.org.

Prayer: *Heavenly Father, I place my faith on the rock of Jesus. He is my foundation as I build a life of obedience and love through Christ's love and in Jesus' name. Amen.*

The Power of Generosity: A generous life for the Lord is built on the foundation of faith in Jesus Christ.

Blessing the Next Generation

Joy is the fruit of a life that sows generosity. Remember those people who made you feel special as a child? They brought a smile to your face and seemed always to be filled with joy and enthusiasm.

Bob MacDonald was that special person to me. Mr. MacDonald lived across the street from my childhood home. He and his wife, Claris, were a compassionate, kind couple. They were generous with their time and attention toward their son, Eddie, who had disabilities, and generous toward me. Mr. MacDonald was a father figure and mentor who gave me the social skills and confidence that allowed me to thrive relationally. Claris enjoyed a Saturday tradition of making chocolate gravy biscuits. I would join them most Saturdays for a generous helping of six to eight cathead biscuits smothered in piping-hot, dark-liquid yumminess!

Soon after my fourteenth birthday, Mr. MacDonald recruited me to work for him during the upcoming summer. Razorback Services (he hailed from Arkansas) was his mom-and-pop company that installed residential garage doors and industrially cleaned tractor trailers and other commercial trucks. It was hot work indeed, and my job was to install two-by-four studs in the sweltering spaces above people's garages. The truck washing was more bearable, with cold water constantly raining down on me.

The winsome way Mr. Mac dealt with homeowners and truck drivers was a life lesson in relational intelligence. He generously loved by looking customers in the eyes, remembering their names, and expressing interest in what interested them. The more I was around Mr. Mac, the more I admired how he generously lived. He was modest about his faith, but I discovered his love for singing in the church choir. I did not attend church at this time, but his generous way of living grew in me a desire to explore my faith. His generosity was modeled after the generous lifestyle of Jesus Christ.

A year after Mr. MacDonald hired me, he and Claris decided to move back to Arkansas. His plan was to sell the garage installation business to my older colleague Earl and the commercial truck washing business to me. As a fifteen-year-old with no credit, Mr. Mac signed a $1,500 loan from our local bank for me to purchase the nascent company from him. I was so nervous and averse to debt that I made sure to pay back the bank in three months.

In the next seven years, along with the help of five friends, I developed and grew the business. Along the way, we earned a degree in the school of hard knocks in how to work with people, how to interpret a profit and loss statement, and how hard work can lead to fulfilling outcomes. I credit the Lord and Bob MacDonald's generous investment in me for what I learned about generous living, maturing as a human being, and valuing faith.

After I embraced faith in Jesus Christ in the spring of my freshman year in college, my wife and I sold the business. We used the proceeds to invest in an out-of-state seminary education. My generous neighbors, Bob and Claris MacDonald, helped point me to the Lord by sowing seeds of generosity and love in my life. In my next season of newfound faith, I experienced God's generous love for me by receiving salvation in his Son, Jesus, and a promise of abundant living to be experienced. Gratitude to God began to ignite my desire for generous living.

The Power of Generosity: Investing our time, expertise, and resources in the next generation reaps the true riches found in God's kingdom.

A Life Given Away

It is impossible to outgive the Lord because, with his almighty influence, he augments any gift we give in Jesus' name. "Give away your life; you'll find life given back, but not merely given back—given back with bonus and blessing. Giving, not getting, is the way. Generosity begets generosity" (Luke 6:37–38 MSG). Eternally motivated gifts grow exponentially. God can take one life surrendered to Jesus and influence a family. He can take a family under the lordship of Christ and influence a church, a ministry, and a community. He can take a Christ-centered community and influence a state. He can take a state that stands for God's principles and revive a nation. Indeed, he has taken a nation founded on his principles and influenced the world. One submitted life is leverage in the Lord's hands. "The generous will themselves be blessed, for they share their food with the poor" (Proverbs 22:9 NIV).

Ralph Waldo Emerson, an American essayist and poet, is credited with saying, "You sow a thought, you reap an action. You sow an action, you reap a habit.

You sow a habit, you reap a character. You sow a character, you reap a destiny." Would you be interested in investing with a 100 percent guaranteed return on your investment? In God's economy, this is how he multiplies gifts given for his glory. He takes our ordinary faith offerings and converts this act of worship into extraordinary eternal results.

When you give in Jesus' name, you are giving to Jesus. The Lord is the righteous recipient of your good and generous gifts. Money is not an end in itself, but there are times when nothing warms the heart like cold cash. Look to give toward faith-based ministries that manage well God's financial resources. Would your giving motivation and amount be any different if you gave to Jesus in person? Would your heart and posture bow in holy reverence and gratitude? Yes, giving is an act of worship to a holy God, not because he needs anything but because we need to recognize our need for him and his reward.

Your Master, Jesus, matches your giving with his incredible resourcefulness and rewards. The Lord has chosen to meet the needs of his people through his people, and he even uses unbelievers to care for believers. And for those outside the faith, it's the kindness of God through godly people that often leads to repentance. Your generous gift combined with God's grace is a conduit for people to know Christ. You cannot outgive God.

Where is the Lord calling you to join him and aggressively give in the name of Jesus?

"If you try to hang on to your life, you will lose it. But if you give up your life for my sake and for the sake of the Good News, you will save it" (Mark 8:35 NLT).

The Power of Generosity: Give away your life to gain your life.

Summary of "Diligent Sower"

- Seeds of love grow to enrich you in every way to be generous in every way.
- When we get down, we must look up and ask the Lord where we can cheerfully give.
- Spontaneous seed sowing reaps unexpected blessings to the giver and the receiver.
- The assurance of your spiritual preparation to meet God after death is a generous gift to your family and those who love you.
- Sowing tears of grief brings comfort and healing to the heart.

- A generous life for the Lord is built on the foundation of faith in Jesus Christ.
- Investing our time, expertise, and resources in the next generation reaps the true riches found in God's kingdom.
- Give away your life to gain your life.

A Generous Prayer

Heavenly Father, I come before you humbly, recognizing the profound truth of sowing and reaping in my life. As I scatter seeds of kindness, let me reap abundant blessings of love and compassion. Grant me wisdom to sow seeds of faith, knowing that in due season, I will reap a harvest of spiritual growth. Help me to sow generously, trusting in your provision, and to reap joyfully, acknowledging your abundant grace. What other seeds of love would you have me sow? May my actions reflect your goodness and may the fruits of my labor bring glory to your name. Amen.

CHAPTER 4

Beyond Blessed

The more you give, the more comes back to you, because God is the greatest giver in the universe, and He won't let you outgive Him.[21]

Randy Alcorn

"Remember the words of the Lord Jesus, how he himself said, 'It is more blessed to give than to receive.'"

Acts 20:35 ESV

How I Am Blessed

Rita Bailey, my wife, reminds me almost every day, "We are beyond blessed!"

As a follower of Jesus Christ, I am beyond blessed with

- grace that is so rich and free,
- love that frees me from fear,
- truth that frees me from lies,
- peace that surpasses my understanding,
- a family who knows me and loves me,
- friends who remind me of Jesus,
- enemies who need my prayers and love,
- a home full of joy,
- clothes to wear,
- food to eat,
- laughter,
- tears,

21 Randy Alcorn, *The Treasure Principle: Discovering the Secret of Joyful Giving* (Multnomah Books, 2001), 73.

- prayers,
- music,
- a mind that is still being renewed,
- a body that is a sacred space for the Lord,
- a soul that is saved, and
- a secure place in heaven!

Together, Rita and I often thank God that we are beyond blessed. We have blessings to share!

Grateful for the Gift of Jesus Christ

Gratitude is a natural launching pad for generosity. At its core, gratitude is being thankful for what God has done through the generous gift on the cross of his Son, Jesus Christ, who offered you salvation by grace through faith and refreshed you with forgiveness of sin and abundant living. "This is how God loved the world: He gave his one and only Son, so that everyone who believes in him will not perish but have eternal life. God sent his Son into the world not to judge the world, but to save the world through him" (John 3:16–17 NLT). Charles Spurgeon painted an emotional picture of God's generous gift for you:

> Look into that face bedewed with bloody sweat for you! Can you not sweat for Him? Look at those hands pierced for you! Shall your hands hang idly down and not be used for Him?
>
> Look at those feet fastened to the wood with nails for you! Can I ask of you any pilgrimage too long to repay the toil which those feet endured for your sake? My Brothers and Sisters, remember what Christ Jesus has done for you! Remember from where He came! Remember the riches which he left! Remember to what He came—the poverty and shame which He endured and how He went down into the depths that He might take us up to the heights!
>
> If you will think of these, you will have the best motive, I think, for beginning to look after His lambs and fighting with those lions which seek to devour His flock. And in that moving motive will be the main means by which you shall be conformed to His image and shall become like He—self-sacrificing—doing your Father's business.[22]

22 Charles Haddon Spurgeon, "The Waterer Watered," sermon delivered April 23, 1865, in *Spurgeon's Sermons*, vol. 11, *1865* (Christian Classics Ethereal Library, n.d.), PDF, 237, https://ccel.org.

Jesus left the riches of heaven to lift us out of our spiritual poverty so we might experience the riches of his grace and mercy. Gratitude for his indescribable, generous gift compels us to generous living!

Prayer: *Heavenly Father, I praise you for giving me your generous love and provision. As I am refreshed by you, I am able to refresh others with a grateful and generous heart. Help me glorify you as I remain faithful to my generous commitments to Christ. I trust you as I wisely give away my time, influence, and affluence. I am at peace knowing that you are faithful and loving to provide for all my needs. Through Christ's love and in Jesus' name. Amen.*

The Power of Generosity: Gratitude begins with the cross of Jesus Christ, where God showed his love for us.

Gratitude Freely Gives

Similarly to our heavenly Father's free gift of salvation in Jesus Christ, so we are called to freely give out of joyful gratitude to those the Lord brings into our lives. The spirit of giving not under compulsion but cheerfully is a theme that flows throughout Scripture.

> The LORD has commanded. Take from among you a contribution to the LORD. Whoever is of a generous heart, let him bring the LORD's contribution....
>
> ...And they came, everyone whose heart stirred him, and everyone whose spirit moved him, and brought the LORD's contribution....All the men and women...brought it as a freewill offering to the LORD. (Exodus 35:4–5, 21, 29 ESV)

The Lord commanded those generous of heart, those whose spirits were moved, to participate in a seasonal freewill offering. This was a special opportunity for God's people to support a project the Lord initiated. This freewill offering was not limited to money but included anything of value that men, women, and children could contribute—freely given to the Lord for his glory. A grateful heart is honored to give to God freely.

Do you freely give, or do you expect something in return? I have to ask myself that question when I spend time or effort on a project or when I'm working with people. My mistake is when I connect my importance or value to the outcomes. This became evident around the time when I was fortysomething. I looked and prayed for younger men to spend time with to encourage them in their faith journey as husbands, dads, and leaders. In the process, I learned as much from them as they learned from me. I also felt a sense of accountability in living out what we discussed; after all, the older man needs to model the way, yes?

I was introduced to a young rising business leader. He was smart and energetic and loved his family and the Lord with fidelity. He asked me to spend time with him and to connect him to my other friends. We enjoyed talking two or three times a week, having dinner with our wives, and attending a silent retreat together. His business flourished, his marriage was strengthened, he became a better dad, and his faith matured. After a year together, with no warning, he decided to cool our relationship and only called when he needed something. At first, I was disappointed and a little confused. Did I do something to disappoint my young friend? Did I become boring? Would those who knew us think I was a failure?

We eventually talked about our relational distance, and I discovered he was grateful for our time together but had discovered new pursuits, friendships, and hobbies. What I learned—and what I am still learning—is to hold with an open hand any relationships, work, finances, and anything else I'm tempted to control. By God's grace, we must resist the urge to control outcomes and especially let go of trying to control other people.

Freely giving is a generous way to live. When we freely give, we give our time, resources, and expertise without expecting anything in return. If one of my mentees asks for accountability to change certain behaviors, like being more intentional with his family, he gives me permission to ask about outcomes. But when we freely give, we leave the results to the Lord. Our gift is to God first and to the person or ministry we support second. God is the overseer of people and resources. His blessing and favor are the indicators of success. So to freely give is to be free from control, to let go, and to trust God with the outcomes.

The Power of Generosity: A grateful heart is honored to give to God freely, not expecting anything in return.

Living in Gratitude, Not Fear

Generous living is more about mindset than money. Because of God's great love for us in giving his Son for the world's salvation, Jesus' followers are joyfully and eternally grateful. An attitude of gratitude governs a generous life. Giving money is only the starting point of being generous, but giving our lives away is God's goal for all those who love him.

What does it mean to live a life of generosity? Every day, everyone we encounter becomes a candidate for our good works since we are responsible managers of what our master Jesus has given us. Generosity flows freely from those who believe blessings are meant to bless others.

In his parable of the talents, Jesus prepared his disciples for their service in kingdom living. "Again, heaven's kingdom is like a wealthy man who went on a long journey and summoned all his trusted servants and assigned his financial management over to them. Before he left on his journey, he entrusted a bag of five thousand gold coins to one of his servants, to another a bag of two thousand gold coins, and to the third a bag of one thousand gold coins, each according to his ability to manage" (Matthew 25:14–15 TPT). Portrayed as the master in the story, Jesus would soon go away to heaven, leaving his servants, the disciples, to steward his money and resources. Two of the three stewards were faithful to courageously and creatively grow their master's assets while the third person did nothing because he was paralyzed by fear. *What if I fail? What if I make my master mad? What if, what if?* The third servant showed no faith or love, only indolence. Faithfulness is rewarded with more while doing nothing leads to the loss of everything.

Astutely, Alexander Maclaren, an eloquent British Baptist preacher from the nineteenth century, described our giving God and how his love moves his children from fear to generosity: "To many men the requirements of religion are more prominent than its gifts, and God is thought of as demanding rather than as 'the giving God.' Such thoughts paralyse action. Fear is barren, love is fruitful.…Fear is a bad reasoner, and the absurd gap between the premises and the conclusion is matched by one of the very same width in every life that thinks of God as rigidly requiring obedience, which, therefore, it does *not* give!"[23]

In contrast with "Fear is a bad reasoner" is such a beautiful truth: Love freely gives and is rewarded with much more to give. Is your life motivated by fear or love? Do you hold on to the Lord's blessings or freely share them? The vistas of your life's potential will open wide the wider you open your hands of generosity for the good of others, not expecting anything in return.

The story Jesus told us about the servants with their master's gold coins is true. This is why we live generously now in preparation for his return. Buried blessings decay and lose their worth while the blessings of time, treasure, and talent that we give away bring people into the way of God. Stay faithful in

23 Alexander Maclaren, "Traders for the Master," in *Expositions of Holy Scripture: St. Matthew Chapters 9 to 28* (S. S. Scranton, 1900), 202.

generous living since love brings others to Jesus. And when he returns or when we go to be with him, he will say, *Enter into the joy of your Lord!*

"Commending his servant, the master replied, 'You have done well, and proven yourself to be my loyal and trustworthy servant. Because you were faithful to manage a small sum, now I will put you in charge of much, much more. You will experience the delight of your master, who will say to you, "Enter into the joy of your Lord!"'" (Matthew 25:23 TPT).

Prayer: *Heavenly Father, grow my heart of gratitude and love so that I can live a generous life through Christ's love. In Jesus' name. Amen.*

The Power of Generosity: Gratitude looks for the possibilities that generosity unearths but fear buries.

During Hard Times

During the COVID-19 lockdown, opportunities abounded to extend generosity through humble service. Not only did generous neighbors of ours practice responsible social distancing by suspending the services of the couple who cleaned their house, but they also still paid them over the nine-month period that they were unable to work. What a beautiful way to show thanksgiving and generous love by supporting those who are unable to work because of the service nature of their profession. A grateful heart tends to well up in generous deeds while trusting God to work things out for the good of everyone. I want to be like our neighbors, showing my gratitude with generous actions.

Paul understood the principle of being grateful for God's incredible blessings in Christ and, out of that overflow of gratitude, of expressing generosity in tangible ways. Paul's desire to refresh the hearts of others with kindness was even more evident in his time of trials and imprisonment. Even in difficulty he experienced the fruit of joy and comfort that flows from a love seeking to serve. As Paul wrote, "I am praying that you will put into action the generosity that comes from your faith as you understand and experience all the good things we have in Christ. Your love has given me much joy and comfort, my brother, for your kindness has often refreshed the hearts of God's people" (Philemon vv. 6–7 NLT). This attitude of gratitude to the Lord for his unspeakable gifts compels us to love out loud. Gratitude to God is an incubator for generosity to God's people. Yes, Jesus refreshes us so that then we are able to refresh others.

In the middle of the COVID-19 monotony, it was so very encouraging to hear the stories of generosity fueled by gratitude and love for people in need around our beloved country. Actor John Krasinski's creative and encouraging video web series, *Some Good News*, highlighted and shared these stories of positivity. Companies repurposed their manufacturing, and many cottage industries blew the dust from old-school sewing machines to produce masks. I'm so proud of my wife for reemploying her stitching skills for this purpose. Teachers paraded their cars through their students' neighborhoods in loving solidarity and care for their community. A crisis brings out the best and the worst in individuals and societies. It was good to see good and generous people serving their neighbors.

During the divinely orchestrated pause the pandemic caused for most of the world, many took the time to be grateful for God's blessings. Some wrote out a gratitude list and read it aloud at mealtime. Others called or texted friends to check on them and thank them for being a significant person in their lives. Wives took time to pen handwritten notes telling husbands how proud they were of them and detailing the joy the husbands brought to their hearts. Grateful husbands described to their wives how they loved and cherished those wives for being patient and forgiving. Fun grandparents video chatted with their grandchildren and read them stories (*The Gruffalo* is a fave with our grands).

Even during difficult times, God gives us more grace so that we can give more grace. The Lord will use your generosity to illustrate the best gift of his Son, Jesus, for the world to trust. "He has given me a new song to sing, a hymn of praise to our God. Many will see what he has done and be amazed. They will put their trust in the LORD" (Psalm 40:3 NLT). Praise to God brings out angels of generosity in God's economy.

Prayer: *Lord, give me a grateful heart that remains generous even in hard times. Help me give selflessly, trusting in your provision and reflecting your love to others. In Jesus' name. Amen.*

The Power of Generosity: Grateful hearts are generous givers, not selfish takers, during difficult days.

Work Like a Doctor, Live Like a Nurse

Generous Giving is a ministry that collects generosity stories from very special people. Renee has one of those unique generosity stories. She is a doctor who earns a physician's income but lives on what a nurse earns. Sound strange? Maybe to some. But through a prayerful process, Renee felt the Lord grow her heart of generosity and eventually led her to a radical result—to live on 25 percent of her salary and give away 75 percent.

Though her generous spirit is instructive, she is the first to warn that this is not prescriptive to everyone but is an invitation for all of us to boldly pray for a heart of radical generosity. God answered his beloved daughter's prayer for wisdom by showing her how abundantly he had blessed her and how she could reallocate some of her earthly investments to heavenly investments. Watching her video story, I learned that she had lost over six figures in a business investment but had a 100 percent return on her kingdom investments.[24]

Renee's spirit of generosity is contagious. Joy exudes from her words, and peace envelops her face when she speaks of the privilege of partnering with the Holy Trinity on her generosity journey. For Renee, the power of generosity is being free from money and status to freely give and serve others. What impressed me most was that her decisions flowed from her time with the Lord as the Holy Spirit led her into her unique journey of generosity. As a doctor, she prescribes that you prayerfully ask your heavenly Father what his generous heart for you looks like and what your generous heart looks like in gratitude to him.

Renee incorporated a very intentional, prayerful giving strategy. What is a giving strategy? Here is my simple definition: "A well-planned, intentional plan for giving based on biblical principles. It empowers people to be more faithful, generous, and fully alive and inspires a legacy of wisdom and generosity for their family."[25]

A grateful heart looks to employ a giving strategy that can be supported by a donor-advised fund, a helpful resource to facilitate and accelerate generosity.

Prayer: *Lord, teach me to live joyfully and gratefully with less so I can give more to those in need. Help me find contentment in simplicity and purpose in generosity. In Jesus' name. Amen.*

The Power of Generosity: Joyfully and gratefully living on less allows us to give away more.

Four Generations of Generous Living

Let me introduce you to a grateful family who has leveraged the NCF donor-advised fund and noncash giving over multiple generations. Ida Bell and I met through a mutual friend. Not long into our first conversation, I was smitten by

24 Renee Lockey, "Work Like a Doctor, Live Like a Nurse," Generous Giving, posted April 9, 2012, Vimeo video, 8:02, https://vimeo.com.

25 For more information, visit https://www.ncfgiving.com.

Ida's genuine heart for generosity. Smitten, as in I wanted to be like Ida. She was gracious with her words and generous with her time by serving on ministry boards. She was generous with her influence as she masterfully connected people and resources so everyone benefited. And she was generous with her resources by investing money and assets in growing Christ-centered initiatives.

What also impressed me about Ida was her keen discernment for how best to resource a start-up ministry. She interviewed me and others at our company Ministry Ventures about a coaching, consulting, and training engagement. In her role on another start-up ministry's board, she took the initiative to sponsor the cost of the executive director to go through the coaching process of learning and implementing the best practices of prayer, board development, ministry plans, operations, and fundraising.

In subsequent meetings, I had the joy of meeting Ida's husband and partner in generosity, Jim. Ida and Jim told me the story of Ida's father, Allen Morris, and how his generous life influenced them as a young married couple to be prayerful and intentional in generous living. Jim and Ida's children, Frank, Allen, and Katie, all became infected with the generational generosity of their parents and grandparents. I have heard each child talk about their parents and grandparents modeling generosity in their everyday lives by helping friends, supporting their church, and giving to missions. Each child experienced their parent's love in unique, generous ways.

Praying as a family for the needs of others and then answering those prayers by giving time and money to help meet those needs, the children saw and experienced their parents' generous love, forgiveness, attention, and joy. Their generous giving was an overflow of their love for God and for people. Now, with their children, Jim and Ida's children are raising and training the fourth generation of generosity.

Having spent time with two of Jim and Ida's grandchildren, James and William, I experienced two young men in their twenties with an authentic passion to love and serve others in generous acts of kindness and through influencing friends by leading Bible studies with them. A culture of generosity continues to flourish in the Bell family thanks to God's grace and the example of each new generation. One recent example blessed my family.

Amy, Frank's wife, heard of Rita's vision of buying a *Pac-Man* video game for our barn, where the grandkids hang out and enjoy table tennis and foosball. The Saturday after our dinner conversation at the Bells, Frank texted and asked if his son, James, and a friend, Daniel, could come by our house. To our amazement and delight, the three generous angels showed up with a brand-new *Pac-Man* video game, unassembled and still in its box.

I hesitated to set it up right away because reading instruction manuals and assembling anything are not my jams! I had nothing to fear though since our generous friends were prepared with a tool belt, battery-powered drill, a can-do attitude, and a lot of know-how. These three servants attached the final panel in fewer than ninety minutes, and presto, lights were flashing, and music was thumping. Who does that? A family with a gene of generosity does. The Bells are a generous family motivated by their generous God to be generous together. Each Bell family member would be the first to say with conviction that God owns all they have and has called them to manage his resources through prayer and generosity.

Prayer: *Lord, help my family grow in gratitude and generosity and unite us with a shared vision that honors you. May our values reflect your love and draw us closer to each other and to you. In Jesus' name. Amen.*

The Power of Generosity: Gratitude and generosity bring families together with a common vision and values that glorify God.

God's Generous Provision, Your Grateful Obedience

Grateful obedience looks for God's generous provision in God's timing while remaining faithful. Scripture preserves a dramatic occasion of three powerful men unable to provide for their armies. Feeling powerless over their drought, the kings inquired of Elisha, the prophet of God, for guidance. Wisely, the leaders turned toward the Lord instead of trying to cover up the crisis. Humility accepts hard realities and confesses total trust in God. Elisha, in the moment, followed the model of his mentor, Elijah.

Before the prophet spoke hard truth to the faces of power, he invited the Spirit to prepare their hearts through public worship of the Lord. While the musicians played melodies in praise to heaven, the hand of the Lord moved the man of God with bold instruction. Then Elisha said, "Thus saith the Lord, Make this valley full of ditches. For thus saith the Lord, Ye shall not see wind, neither shall ye see rain; yet that valley shall be filled with water, that ye may drink, both ye, and your cattle, and your beasts" (2 Kings 3:16–17 KJV). Swiftly, the men desperate for God obediently dug ditches, and the Lord filled them with water. Following their grateful obedience, God's generosity provided more than enough.

What is God asking you to do? Be assured that whatever the Lord is leading you to do, it is best for you. Remember, his divine request may require significant effort with unclear outcomes, so work with an eye of faith fixed on the faithfulness of your heavenly Father. His ways, though not your ways, are still the best in the long term.

Temptations and disobedience can distract you, so be aware of short-term solutions that only result in morsels instead of the Spirit's fruitful abundance. It is more fulfilling to remain faithful in the arduous work of digging and removing obstacles and then be able to marvel with amazement at God's unconventional provision. His glory is assured when you follow his sure path, one step of obedience at a time. He provides. Jesus embraced a life of faithfulness by humbling himself and becoming a servant who lived an obedient life, who died on the cross, and whose name the Lord has highly exalted above all names.

Jesus "made himself of no reputation, and took upon him the form of a servant, and was made in the likeness of men: And being found in fashion as a man, he humbled himself, and became obedient unto death, even the death of the cross. Wherefore God also hath highly exalted him, and given him a name which is above every name" (Philippians 2:7–9 KJV).

Perhaps there is a blessing of provision waiting to follow your obedience. Stay in the process. Though it may seem like you are shoveling hard soil, the exertion of your emotional and physical energy is not in vain. Digging dirt is dirty, sweaty, and not a fun experience, but God's provision will follow your faithfulness. Invite in often the praise and worship of God's people to point your heart to your generous provider, God the Father, Son, and Spirit. Abundant provision of forgiveness, peace, and security await your humble heart. Your divine owners, the Holy Trinity, may direct you to increase your giving so your heart of faith, love, and hope grows even stronger in uncertain days. Bountiful blessings of provision await your loving obedience to do the next brave thing.

Charles Spurgeon described with beauty and boldness our preparation and God's provision: "If we expect to obtain the Holy Spirit's blessing, we must prepare for his reception. 'Make this valley full of trenches' is an order which is given me this morning for the members of this church; make ready for the Holy Ghost's power; be prepared to receive that which he is about to give; each man in his place and each woman in her sphere, make the whole of this church full of trenches for the reception of the divine waterfloods."[26]

26 Charles Haddon Spurgeon, "Make This Valley Full of Ditches," The Spurgeon Center for Biblical Preaching at Midwestern Seminary, sermon given April 28, 1867, https://www.spurgeon.org.

Your obedient preparation invites the Holy Spirit to fill you with all wisdom, strength, and joy! "Be filled with the Spirit; speaking to yourselves in psalms and hymns and spiritual songs, singing and making melody in your heart to the Lord; giving thanks always for all things unto God and the Father in the name of our Lord Jesus Christ; submitting yourselves one to another in the fear of God" (Ephesians 5:18–21 KJV).

Prayer: *Heavenly Father, give me the faith and perseverance to do the hard things through Christ's love and in Jesus' name. Amen.*

The Power of Generosity: A grateful heart joyfully obeys the Lord and trusts in him to provide.

The Business Owner and the Fisherman

Our part is to take the next step of faith, and the Lord's part is to provide in his timing. We will close this chapter with two contrasting mindsets: One is never satisfied, rarely grateful, and driven for more, and the other is beyond blessed, always grateful, and content with today.

In a bustling city, there lived a merchant named Robert. His wealth was vast, and his business ventures spanned many lands. His grand house was adorned with the finest treasures, and his table always overflowed with the best foods. Despite his prosperity, Robert found himself troubled, for with great wealth came great burdens. At night, he worried about his investments, and during the day, the demands of managing his riches consumed him.

One day, as Robert walked along the shore to clear his mind, he encountered a fisherman named Michael. Michael's boat was modest, and he caught few fish, but he sang as he mended his nets. Intrigued by the fisherman's apparent contentment, Robert approached him and asked, "Why do you sing so joyfully? Your possessions are few, and your life seems hard."

Michael looked up and smiled. "I sing because I have all I need. My family is healthy, my needs are met, and my heart is at peace. I trust in God's provision."

Robert pondered Michael's words and invited him to his grand house. He showed Michael his wealth and said, "With all this, I am not content. How can one with so little be so happy?"

Michael replied, "Wealth provides security and comfort, but it can also ensnare you with worry and greed. True contentment comes not from the abundance of possessions but from a content heart."

That night, Robert lay in his lavish bed, unable to sleep. He thought of Michael's simple life and the joy that radiated from him. The next morning, Robert sought out Michael again and asked, "Teach me your ways so I might find peace."

Michael took Robert out in his boat. As they worked side by side, Robert began to understand the value of simplicity and the joy found in labor free from wealth's constant pull. He discovered that his pursuit of more had robbed him of true contentment. In time, Robert learned to simplify his life. Instead of pursuing only wealth, he gave generously to those in need and spent more time with his family. His anxiety lessened, and he found peace when he trusted God for his provision.

Solomon, the wealthiest person of his day, once wrote, "Better is a little with the fear of the Lord than great treasure and trouble with it" (Proverbs 15:16 ESV). Robert realized this truth: Wealth, though beneficial, must not overshadow the simple joys of life or our trust in God. Robert lived the rest of his days with a grateful heart, knowing that true wealth is measured not in possessions but in joy, peace, and generous living.

Summary of "Beyond Blessed"

- Gratitude begins with the cross of Jesus Christ, where God showed his love for us.
- A grateful heart is honored to give to God freely, not expecting anything in return.
- Gratitude looks for the possibilities that generosity unearths but fear buries.
- Grateful hearts are generous givers, not selfish takers, during difficult days.
- Joyfully and gratefully living on less allows us to give away more.
- Gratitude and generosity bring families together with a common vision and values that glorify God.
- A grateful heart joyfully obeys the Lord and trusts in him to provide.

A Generous Prayer

Lord, I am humbled by your boundless generosity. In your grace, you shower blessings on me daily. Thank you for the gift of life, for every breath I take is a testament to your love. Your provision knows no bounds, and it sustains me through trials and triumphs. In moments of doubt, your presence brings solace, guiding me along your path. I am grateful for your mercy, which forgives my shortcomings and offers redemption. What little blessings am I overlooking that I can praise you for in a big way? Out of the overflow of my grateful heart, how can I reflect your generous love and kindness to others? Amen.

PART 2

Generosity Practices

What are generosity practices? They are simply everyday habits we cultivate into a way of life—a life of generous living. Generosity practices are intentional ways of living so that we become the best version of the person God wants us to become. As John Mark Comer explained, such practices are a rule of life: "A Rule of Life is *a schedule and set of practices and relational rhythms that create space for us to be with Jesus, become like him, and do as he did, as we live in alignment with our deepest desires*. It's a way of intentionally organizing our lives around what matters most: God."[27] The purpose of generosity practices is to make them a rule of life for the Lord to rule over our life in love and generosity.

Over the next four chapters, we will explore the generosity practices of creating sacred spaces, being relationally intentional, serving humbly, and living generously.

---

27 John Mark Comer, *Practicing the Way: Be with Jesus. Become like Him. Do as He Did.* (WaterBrook, 2024), 161.

CHAPTER 5

Creating Sacred Spaces

God is both further from us, and nearer to us, than any other being.[28]

C. S. Lewis

"Be still, and know that I am God."

Psalm 46:10 NIV

What Are Sacred Spaces?

Sacred spaces are environments that allow us to sense God's love for us more powerfully. Silence, solitude, and stillness all work together to center the soul on the love of the Father, Son, and Holy Spirit. When we give ourselves permission to experience God in sacred spaces, we are generous to our souls. Being generous to our souls means nurturing our spiritual health with time, prayer, rest, and practices that draw us closer to God. In my walk with Christ, when I neglect spending time in sacred spaces, my soul shrivels due to lack of love. However, in the seasons of life when lingering in sacred places is part of my normal rhythm, like eating, sleeping, and breathing, my soul sings. And in a singing soul is found the melody of a generous life. Here are some ideas on how to compose the lyrics of your life so you sing a song of grateful generosity to God. Give yourself permission to be generous in creating sacred spaces.

Silent Retreats

Beth Bennett is passionate about creating sacred spaces and is an expert at leading silent retreats. She is also a gifted nonprofit consultant who helps organizations with their prayer strategies, board development, ministry plans, administration, and fundraising. She serves dedicated, God-called servant

28 C. S. Lewis, *The Problem of Pain* (HarperOne, 2001), 33.

leaders who sometimes drift into substituting their devotion to Christ with their service for Christ. Taking God's grace for granted can cause sacred spaces to seem dull. Prayer can feel like self-talk, and the Bible can seem uninspiring. We can lose our focus on loving God and people.

Because Beth has experienced her own season of burnout, she recognizes when people need an infusion of sacred spaces. Chronic exhaustion, anger, judgmental attitudes, and readiness to quit are all evidence of a needy soul. Beth is passionate about expanding her sacred spaces, so she is enthusiastic to help others romance the Trinity through silence, solitude, and stillness. She is generous in her personal time with God so she can facilitate days of silence for those eager to hear the loving voice of their Lord. Silence is the language of God. We immerse ourselves in silence to learn how to become fluent in being loved by our heavenly Father as his beloved child.

A silent retreat offers a unique opportunity to withdraw from the noise of daily life and enter a place of quiet reflection. In silence, we make space for God's voice to rise above our inner and outer distractions. This practice aligns with Jesus' example: he often retreated to solitary places to pray, find strength, and renew his spirit. When we silence our environment and our minds, we open ourselves to hear God more clearly, to reconnect with our purpose, and to reflect on his Word without interruption.

Here are some benefits we experience during a silent retreat. In this stillness, we can examine our thoughts and emotions before God, letting go of stress and finding peace. We may even gain insight into areas of our lives where he's calling us to change. Above all, silence allows us to experience God's presence deeply, fostering a renewed sense of clarity, purpose, and spiritual growth. The common theme for my time investment in protracted silence is experiencing God's love.

Because of Beth's example and her admonition to slow down, silent retreats have become a staple for my spiritual development. Five of us in our Finishing Well accountability group recently attended a three-day silent retreat. Our accountability group meets monthly for three hours to share life updates, especially those related to our spiritual and relational life. The outcome for me was the same as the previous twenty or so silent retreats I had experienced: the still, small voice of Love reassuring me, *Boyd, I love you for who I have created you to be, my beloved son whom I have called and equipped to love others in my name. Stay secure in my love for you, and I will give you the capacity to care for and serve people. Rest. Relax. And let my love restore your soul. Even with what you control,*

I still create the outcomes. Trust me. Love me. Worship me. Surrender all, submit all, and I will give you all you need.

At the end of my retreat, my soul was flush with faith, and God also refreshed my friends. Solitude and silence position us to hear God, as 1 Kings 19:11–12 highlights: "The Lord passed by [Elijah], and a great and strong wind tore into the mountains and broke the rocks in pieces before the Lord, but the Lord was not in the wind; and after the wind an earthquake, but the Lord was not in the earthquake; and after the earthquake a fire, but the Lord was not in the fire; and after the fire a still small voice" (NKJV).

Henri Nouwen wisely pointed out that Elijah needed to be reminded how to hear the Lord:

> Solitude is not a solution. It is a direction. The direction is pointed to by the prophet Elijah, who did not find Yahweh in the mighty wind, the earthquake, the fire, but in the still, small voice; this direction, too, is indicated by Jesus, who chose solitude as the place to be with his Father. Every time we enter into solitude we withdraw from our windy, earthquaking, fiery lives and open ourselves to the great encounter. The first thing we often discover in solitude is our own restlessness, our drivenness, and compulsiveness, our urge to act quickly, to make an impact, and to have influence; and often we find it very hard to withstand the temptation to return as quickly as possible to the world of "relevance." But when we persevere with the help of a gentle discipline, we slowly come to hear the still, small voice and to feel the gentle breeze, and so come to know the Lord of our heart, soul, and mind, the Lord who makes us see who we really are.[29]

Indeed, it is so true. It's like silence detoxes us from distractions to truly hear God's heart.

God's Home

Next let me introduce you to another special couple who is creating sacred spaces to inspire and instruct others in silent retreats. Larry and Jody Green have created sacred spaces for themselves and gatherings of twenty to thirty people in three-day directed silent retreats for over twenty years. Participants hear teachings on prayer and spiritual formation followed by time for individual

29 Henri Nouwen, "Open Yourself to the Great Encounter," Henri Nouwen Society, March 17, 2024, https://henrinouwen.org.

reflection in stillness and silence, listening for the Lord's customized love for them. Retreat attendees come away refreshed by God's love, and many times, they receive a clarifying word of the Lord's will for their lives.

Several years ago, because Larry and Jody lived three hours away from an adequate prayer retreat facility, they began to pray for a closer option. Through the process of prayer and a series of God stories, a picturesque two hundred acres nestled in the Appalachian foothills of northern Georgia became God's Home. Through the generosity of God's people, Larry and Jody secured and developed the land, including the construction of a prayer chapel and accommodations for six people to stay overnight. This sacred space has already blessed dozens of Jesus' disciples by giving them a special space to feel God's love more intimately. Silence, solitude, and stillness are gifts to be received and enjoyed by those intent on growing in their relationship with the Father, Son, and Spirit. God's Home is one of his gifts to be joyfully experienced.[30]

When we immerse ourselves in silence, we allow God's love to fill us, nurture our souls, and help us grow in empathy and compassion. This experience invites us to share that generous love with others in meaningful ways.

Practicing this generous love can start with a practice we can all incorporate as a way of life: intentional listening—being fully present with others and valuing their stories. Offering our time, even when busy, is another powerful gesture. Simple acts demonstrate love, like preparing a meal, offering a kind word, or reaching out to someone who may be lonely. We can also pray for others, even silently, lifting their needs to God. As we grow in love through silence, we become more attuned to ways we can serve and bless those around us.

Prayer: *Lord, in the quiet, I feel your generous love surround me. Teach me to embrace silence, the Spirit's language, so that I may become fluent in your love and share it freely. In Jesus' name. Amen.*

The Power of Generosity: God's generous love is experienced in silence, the language of the Holy Spirit. Immersion in silence helps us become fluent in the Lord's love.

A Spiritual Director

Another option for creating a sacred space is meeting with a spiritual director. A spiritual director is a guide who helps you grow closer to Christ. The best ones are gifted listeners who ask soul-jarring questions to help you discover God's

30 For more information, visit https://cloudwalk.org/gods-home/.

heart for you. Allow me to share a little about Tom Ashbrook, my spiritual director.

I read Tom Ashbrook's book *Mansions of the Heart*[31] in my early fifties, just after completing treatment for early-stage prostate cancer. I was spiritually, emotionally, and physically exhausted, needing my heavenly Father's comfort and love. I was longing for a deeper walk with Christ. My soul thirsted for intimacy with my Father. I knew in my heart that I was his beloved son on whom his favor rested, but I needed rest. My tender heart needed a fresh infusion of my Savior's generous encouragement and the Spirit's healing.

Tom's book was a catalyst for the Spirit to reveal his love and dispel my fears. *Mansions of the Heart* is based on Saint Teresa of Ávila's monumental work from the sixteenth century, *The Interior Castle*. The focus of both books is oneness with God's love for the child of God, moving beyond just doing for the Lord to being with the Lord. These divinely inspired ideas gave me permission to be still and, in the process, ignited my spiritual imagination during a weeklong silent retreat at the Abbey of the Genesee outside Rochester, New York.

In my utter excitement, I called Tom to thank him for his impactful book, and in the course of our conversation, he invited me to join him for a weeklong seminar he was leading in Phoenix that fall. Since two of our daughters lived in Phoenix, it was not hard to convince Rita to join me for a spiritual pilgrimage to spend time with Jesus, Bethany, and Anna. That week, I was the first to arrive and the last to leave. Tom kept me engaged with his honesty about his own spiritual struggles and the reminder of the generous access we have to God's love. It was a sacred space, indeed, for my heart to hear the truth.

A decade later, Tom and I reunited at a men's conference in Canada. Over lunch, I mentioned to him my three-year quest for a spiritual director. I asked Tom if he was interested and available to serve in this capacity. He was! So for almost three years, we have engaged in a monthly ninety-minute Zoom call. During each call, he graciously guides me to God's lavish love that longs to embrace me, the Lord's beloved son in whom he is well pleased. Tom and I laugh and cry each time we get together. His generous investment in my spiritual formation has deepened my love for the Father, Son, and Spirit and expanded my capacity to love people. A spiritual director helps us grow in our intimacy and oneness in God's love.

31 Tom Ashbrook, *Mansions of the Heart: Exploring the Seven Stages of Spiritual Growth* (Jossey-Bass, 2009).

Prayer: *Lord, thank you for the gift of guidance. As I invest time with my spiritual mentor, deepen my intimacy with you, drawing me closer into the oneness of your love. In Jesus' name. Amen.*

The Power of Generosity: Time invested with a spiritual guide grows our intimacy and oneness in God's love.

Fast from Screens

Reducing screen time can feel like a challenge, especially in a world where screens have become central to work, relationships, and entertainment. Yet making intentional choices to cut back on screen time can open space for richer, more meaningful connections and create opportunities to be generous in new ways. Here are practical steps to reduce screen time and the benefits that can flow from this choice:

1. **Set Boundaries for Device Use:** Start by establishing clear boundaries. Limit screen time to specific hours, like after work or not during meals or family time. Use your phone's Do Not Disturb or screen-time features to help track usage and remind you of your goals. By limiting screen use, you'll free up time to be present with others, offering your full attention, which is one of the most generous gifts you can give.
2. **Engage in Hobbies Without Screens:** Instead of reaching for a phone or watching TV, consider engaging in hobbies that don't involve screens. Reading a physical book, crafting, cooking, or even doing outdoor activities can help you rediscover the joy of real-world engagement. Investing time in meaningful activities can inspire you to share your skills or creations with others, like preparing a home-cooked meal for a friend or volunteering your talents to help someone in need.
3. **Replace Scrolling with Serving:** Instead of spending an hour scrolling on social media, consider dedicating that time to serving others. Visit someone who may need encouragement, help a neighbor, or volunteer at a local charity. You might also find that this shift frees up resources. For instance, by spending less on entertainment subscriptions or screen-driven purchases, you have more to donate or invest in causes that matter to you.

4. **Practice Digital Sabbaths:** Set aside one day a week where you go screen-free. Use this time for reflection, prayer, or quality time with loved ones. As you experience the benefits, you'll find yourself more rested and available to respond generously to others, whether through offering your undivided attention, sharing your resources, or extending a helping hand.

As we reduce screen time, we free up not only our hours but also our hearts. With more mental clarity, we can be intentional about using our influence for good and offering encouragement and positivity. Reducing screen time helps us become more aware of the world around us as we generously use our time, money, resources, and attention and build deeper relationships so we can live out our faith in tangible, impactful ways.

Prayer: *Lord, help me reduce my screen time, freeing my heart and mind to be more present and generous with my time, attention, and love for others. In Jesus' name. Amen.*

The Power of Generosity: Decreased screen time increases our capacity for generosity.

Sacred Space for a Generous Community

A community of generosity is a gathering of people committed to sharing God's love, time, resources, and encouragement with one another and the world. Rooted in Jesus' teachings, such a community is marked by a spirit of giving that reflects God's own generosity. This type of community doesn't just give; it overflows with kindness, support, and encouragement, creating an environment where people thrive spiritually, emotionally, and even materially. Engaging with a community of generous followers of Christ brings incredible benefits, enriching us and inspiring us to give more freely to others. Here are five ways we benefit from being part of such a community:

1. **Spiritual Growth and Encouragement:** In a generous community, believers encourage each other in their faith journey. When we share our testimonies, victories, and even struggles, we help one another grow closer to Christ. The early church embodied this, gathering to pray, study, and support one another (Acts 2:42–47). By surrounding ourselves with people who share and live out their faith, we gain encouragement to pursue our

own spiritual growth. We receive reminders of God's faithfulness and are strengthened in our commitment to follow him.

2. **Emotional Support During Difficult Times:** Life brings hardships, and having a community of generous believers to lean on during those times is invaluable. When one person in a generous community is in need, others are quick to respond with prayers, presence, and practical help. Generosity in a Christ-centered community often means showing up for each other, sharing burdens, and providing comfort. This support fosters emotional resilience, reminding us that we're not alone. As we receive care, we also learn to be generous with our compassion, extending the same comfort to others when they're in need.
3. **Practical Assistance in Times of Need:** In a generous community, people share not only their spiritual lives but also their material resources. Followers of Jesus give what they have to help meet the needs of others, following the example of the early church, where believers shared their possessions so that no one lacked (Acts 4:32–35). When you're part of a community like this, you benefit from practical support during difficult times, whether it's financial assistance, meals during a crisis, or help with day-to-day tasks. This practical generosity shows God's love in tangible ways and teaches us to rely on him to meet our needs through his people.
4. **A Sense of Belonging and Purpose:** Generous communities cultivate a strong sense of belonging and purpose. In these communities, everyone has a role, and each person's gifts are valued and used for the good of others. By engaging in acts of service—whether by helping with church events, mentoring younger members, or participating in outreach—we feel deeply connected and purposeful. This purpose extends beyond the group, empowering us to share God's love more openly with the world. Knowing that we're part of something larger than ourselves, we experience the fulfillment that comes from contributing to God's work and building his kingdom.
5. **Learning to Live Generously:** Being surrounded by generous believers teaches us to adopt a lifestyle of giving. In a community

> that prioritizes generosity, we see examples of sacrificial giving and acts of kindness daily. These examples inspire us to become more openhanded, to serve without expecting anything in return, and to view all we have as God's to use. We learn that generosity isn't just about money; it's also about giving our time, attention, and care to others. As we learn to give more freely, we experience the joy that comes from living generously—a joy that deepens our relationship with God and others.

In a world often marked by self-focus and scarcity, a community of generosity shines as a powerful witness of Christ's love. We become part of something that mirrors God's kingdom, where no one is in need, where love abounds, and where everyone is valued. This type of community enriches our lives and empowers us to give more fully to others, trusting that God's love and provision will always sustain us.

By engaging in a community of generous followers of Jesus, we grow in faith, experience support, and learn what it truly means to give. As the generosity of others blesses us, we're inspired to live out that same generosity in our own lives, reflecting Christ's love to the world.

Prayer: *Lord, thank you for the blessing of a generous community. Help me embrace their love and support and inspire me to share your kindness and generosity with others. In Jesus' name. Amen.*

The Power of Generosity: Living in a community of generosity inspires and instructs generosity.

Sacred Hospitality Space

The gospel of Luke paints the Christmas story as a picture of humble beginnings. Amid the bustling town of Bethlehem, a harried innkeeper found himself approached by yet another weary couple seeking shelter. This narrative, though brief, resonates profoundly with the themes of generosity and hospitality as the innkeeper played the simple yet profound role in the birth of Jesus. The businessman, likely inundated with guests due to the census (think Taylor Swift concert in town), had no grand accommodations to offer Mary and Joseph. Yet, recognizing their need, he didn't turn them away. His generosity and compassion shone through as he provided them with what little space he had available—a humble stable. Within these modest surroundings, the Savior of the world entered humanity. "She gave birth to her firstborn son and wrapped him in swaddling cloths and laid him in a manger, because there was no place for them in the inn" (Luke 2:7 ESV). God blesses what we have when we give it to him for his purposes. What seems meager may glorify the Lord the most.

What appears to be an insignificant gift from this seemingly minor character in the nativity story actually emphasizes the providential arrangement of God's plan unfolding in the most unassuming circumstances. In this simple act of providing shelter, the kind entrepreneur unknowingly played a pivotal role in fulfilling ancient prophecies. He welcomed the birth of the long-awaited Messiah, showcasing a heart willing to extend hospitality and care even in the most meager of settings. What a beautiful expression of generous resourcefulness in a difficult situation.

The innkeeper's example resonates profoundly with the church's understanding regarding the importance of hospitality and generosity. Martin Luther, for instance, stressed the Christian duty of helping our neighbors in need, emphasizing that even the smallest acts of kindness reflect Christ's love. This innkeeper's generosity echoed the spirit of Christ's teachings, emphasizing the value of selflessness and compassion. His provision of a stable, though a simple gesture, showcased a heart open to serving others and meeting their needs, embodying the essence of following Jesus. You may feel that you are full to capacity, but ask the Lord for other creative alternatives. Like the innkeeper, look beyond traditional means to innovative ideas that may actually be better.

Your selfless gesture could be part of the fulfillment of God's plan, demonstrating that no act of kindness done in the name of love goes unnoticed in God's sight. As you celebrate the birth, life, death, and resurrection of Jesus, reflect on being generous with who you are and what you have. By God's grace, emulate a spirit of hospitality and selflessness, opening your hearts to extend kindness and care to those in need. In doing so, you follow in the footsteps of the innkeeper by welcoming Christ into your life through acts of love and generosity toward others. Instead of telling a blunt no to someone in need, consider a "not right now" or offer alternatives for other relationships or resources that may even be superior. Use warm hospitality to welcome Jesus and all those who need his love.

Prayer: *Heavenly Father, show me your creative heart of generosity when I feel like I have nothing to offer to others in need. Through Christ's love and in Jesus' name. Amen.*

The Power of Generosity: Creative options for generosity can reveal ways to love others with resources that we already have available.

Sacred Space for Loved Ones

Our homes can be a sanctuary of healing and hope for those we love the most. One compelling example is Katrina, a friend I have worked with over the years at the National Christian Foundation, who is a harnessed hurricane of love and generosity. I admire her other-centered living and her heart for others. She loves so well for Jesus.

One example of her generous love occurred around ten years ago when she invited her daughter, Amy, and her new son-in-law, Wayne, to live in her home so they could save money for a down payment on their own home. What began as a one- or two-year experiment became a ten-year one as the young couple struggled to gather enough resources. But in the process of being together longer than anticipated, they went deeper into their love for one another and for the Lord. No doubt they were impacted by being around Katrina. For Wayne, it is certain that his mother-in-law rubbed off on him since he began to talk about God with his family and even take the lead to offer prayers.

One example of a positive influence on this young couple was Katrina's generous prayers. Wayne was looking for a job that would allow his family to move into their own home. Wayne's work was in a feast-or-famine industry, and he worked for himself. So his income was sporadic and unpredictable. One day, Amy asked Wayne if he had prayed about his job situation. Wayne thought about it for a minute and said he just realized that, in fact, he had not. He had been trying to figure out what to do on his own. So Wayne began to pray and asked Katrina, Amy, and others to pray with him and for him. In community, they prayed for the Lord to open a door for a new job for Wayne.

Moments after Wayne's prayer asking for the Lord's guidance in his job search, his stepbrother called him and asked if he was interested in working at his company. It just so happened that his employer was in the same industry that Wayne worked in, but this job would be on a salary basis with consistent pay, about twice as much as he was used to being paid. And now, through the grace of Jesus Christ, Wayne is not only providing a home for his own family but has become a financial blessing for his mother-in-law as well. Thank you, Jesus!

What touched me about this precious family was Katrina's generosity in hosting and serving her daughter, son-in-law, and grandchild for such a long period of time. Instead of complaining, she saw the blessing of being together. Being in proximity to her adult children and grandbaby increased her influence with them. Even more than the financial benefit was the spiritual benefit for this young couple, who were influenced by Katrina's generous life. What a celebration of how God used a mother's generosity to create a sacred space in her home to care for those she loved most.

The Power of Generosity: What seems like a life interruption may be a convenient way to generously love others like Jesus does.

Sacred Space for Healing

A home is also able to offer the hospitality of healing when the healing of Jesus is experienced on an ongoing basis. Home can be a sanctuary of hope where bodies can mend, emotions can heal, and relationships can repair. As we see in Mark, "Simon's mother-in-law was in bed with a fever, and they immediately told Jesus about her. So he went to her, took her hand and helped her up. The fever left her and she began to wait on them" (1:30–31 NIV).

Simon Peter invited Jesus to come into his home to help his mother-in-law, who was sick with a fever. The rugged fisherman was not only the breadwinner of his home but also the compassionate son-in-law who made sure to take care of his wife's mom. Not one to ever be shy about taking action, impetuous Peter knew Jesus could make a difference in his home, especially in the physical affairs of his mother-in-law. With a simple touch, Jesus healed her, and she began to serve them. Peter had left home to follow Jesus, but when his home was in need, he came home to give Jesus.

A home that often invites Jesus in for fellowship and healing is a home whose safe environment extends hope to anxious minds, love to fearful souls, and mercy to broken hearts. A home with a healing atmosphere recognizes that Jesus will only enter if invited. Jesus saves us from sin and hell, bringing heaven on earth. Hospitality is where Christ's love prevails. It heals, freeing the healthy to serve. "Share with the Lord's people who are in need. Practice hospitality" (Romans 12:13 NIV).

You can start by making sure your home is a place for spiritual, emotional, and relational healing so you are prepared to offer the hospitality gift of healing. This first step is to make sure you, your family, and God are connected in love and trust. With the Lord's help, you have forgiven pain from past hurts, let go of grudges, and ended resentment's ugly influence. You are healed when you confess your pain to Jesus and apply his healing forgiveness. You can experience healing when the righteous prayers of friends cover your brokenness, mending and molding you back to your healthy self. You heal your spouse by listening with empathy and responding with compassionate care. You heal your children with hugs of hope, reminding them of your love, even when they make bad choices. When your home is healed, you qualify as a haven of hospitality to offer healing, hope, and safety to others.

A healthy home accepts uniqueness, affirms value, and, in love, keeps fear at bay or sends it away. Maybe a child in your life does not have a loving parent available to protect them and train them in the ways of the Lord. For a season, Christ may be calling you to be the child's home of healing so that one day, they will be blessed with a healthy home of their own. Or maybe children in your community are hungry to learn the Bible. You can be their conduit to learn about Christ with fun activities, Bible reading, and Scripture memory. Feed them, and they will come—the Jesus method! Perhaps once a month, you host meals in your home with extended family. Take the initiative to serve how the Lord leads.

Your hospitality of healing is a priceless gift to all hurting hearts. "Offer hospitality to one another without grumbling" (1 Peter 4:9 NIV).

Prayer: *Heavenly Father, bring healing to our home so we, in turn, can offer our home as a sanctuary of healing to hurting hearts. Through Christ's love and in Jesus' name. Amen.*

The Power of Generosity: Healing happens in a home that invites in Jesus for his healing touch.

Sacred Space to Serve Globally

I met Scott Bowen when he was a strapping seventeen-year-old lad. After Scott graduated from college, he worked for his dad, learning how to serve people well and manage a business. However, when Scott paused to pray and contemplate his calling, he felt a holy discontent. The Holy Spirit was nudging him toward a more direct kingdom focus. Scott was faithful to love and encourage those in the construction industry but sensed God calling him to something more.

A friend invited Scott to Uganda on a mission trip, and *wham*, he fell in love with getting to know and serve the young boys he met there. Scott quickly learned that soccer was the national sport and passion of teenage boys. Sadly, though, the fields lacked a smooth grass-covered surface to play a quality soccer game. The fields and equipment were neglected and unkempt, and the rough ground was littered with rocks and bare patches. The balls, nets, and jerseys were secondhand, tired, and worn out. Scott felt sad at the overwhelming human needs but was glad he was there to help. He experienced a heavenly fire erupting in his heart to love these young men to Jesus through sports.

Scott came home to the US but felt compelled by the Lord to go back. He enthusiastically shared with his dad the vision of using soccer for outreach and discipleship. Howard lovingly listened to his son and wisely advised him to pray and see what God would do. He reassured Scott that he would support whatever career direction God was leading him to serve. Like Abraham trusting Isaac to the Lord, Howard entrusted Scott to their heavenly Father. As an earthly father, Howard had hoped Scott would follow him in the construction business but knew his heavenly Father's heart was for him to hold his father-son relationship with an open hand.

Scott expressed to me his passion with fierce emotion, saying, "On my trips to Uganda, the thing God put on my heart was this burden to see that these middle and high school boys who didn't have strong connections with their fathers could experience healthy male role models in the form of coaches. Because I was truly burdened to see these boys connected to a strong male influence during the formative years of middle and high school, I was compelled by God's generous love to take action."

As time passed, Scott's heart was confirmed by God's call to serve overseas. Scripture, godly counsel, and his parents' support clarified and confirmed the Lord's will. Scott took what he learned from the construction business and applied the skills to purchase land in Uganda, build soccer fields, and manage local leaders in a new ministry called Champions United. Champions United's sports fields not only were the best in the community but were also celebrated as the best in the entire country. Most compelling to the generous givers who helped start the organization was its financial sustainability. Currently, local clubs, teams, and other groups from around the country pay rental income that covers the cost of maintaining the fields and equipment, and local leaders are paid to mentor the boys.

Since Scott's initial vision for Champions United, God has blessed them with ten soccer fields throughout Uganda, with five thousand young men annually learning about Jesus and leadership.[32] Mature mentors of the faith teach these young men the ways of the Lord. These fields have become sacred spaces in Uganda.

Creating sacred spaces to mentor these young men is a powerful way to guide them in faith, shaping them into mature men of God. In a safe, supportive

32 For more information, visit https://www.championsunitedfc.org.

environment, they can openly explore questions, express doubts, and learn from those who have walked the path before them. These spaces allow mentors to share wisdom, teach values, and model Christlike behavior, encouraging young men to grow deeper in their relationship with God.

As they are taught to ground their identity in Christ, young men learn the importance of integrity, responsibility, and humility. This nurturing environment provides a foundation for spiritual maturity and empowerment to live out their faith boldly. Through mentorship, young men become equipped to face life's challenges with faith and purpose and to embody God's love in the world.

Scott's story is an illustration of the letting loose of earthly attachments and embracing heavenly treasures. Instead of feeling stuck in the mold of someone else's expectations, he followed the path of generosity, which included making disciples of those from another culture. Scott's affection for Jesus Christ far exceeded his love for the world. Generosity is the overflow of a life wholeheartedly in love with Jesus—a life generously sending treasures ahead to heaven.

Prayer: *Lord, lead me on the great adventure of giving my life for others. Help me discover true purpose and joy as I serve and follow you. In Jesus' name. Amen.*

The Power of Generosity: Follow God on the great adventure of giving your life away for others, and in the process, you will find your life.

Summary of "Creating Sacred Spaces"

- God's generous love is experienced in silence, the language of the Holy Spirit. Immersion in silence helps us become fluent in the Lord's love.
- Time invested with a spiritual guide grows our intimacy and oneness in God's love.
- Decreased screen time increases our capacity for generosity.
- Living in a community of generosity inspires and instructs generosity.
- Creative options for generosity can reveal ways to love others with resources that we already have available.
- What seems like a life interruption may be a convenient way to generously love others like Jesus does.

- Healing happens in a home that invites in Jesus for his healing touch.
- Follow God on the great adventure of giving your life away for others, and in the process, you will find your life.

A Generous Prayer

Lord, thank you for sacred spaces where I find you in silence, where stillness allows your voice to fill my heart. With the guidance of a spiritual director, I uncover deeper truths and grow in wisdom. In my community of generosity, I feel your love shared through the kindness and support of others, teaching me the beauty of giving and receiving. And in serving those around me, I experience your presence in the act of selflessness, and I learn to see you in each person I encounter. Draw me ever closer in these sacred spaces and shape me into your image. May each encounter, each quiet moment, and each act of service deepen my intimacy with you and strengthen my faith. In Jesus' name. Amen.

CHAPTER 6

Being Relationally Intentional

You can get everything in life you want,
if you help enough other people get what they want.[33]
Zig Ziglar

Walk with the wise and become wise,
for a companion of fools suffers harm.
Proverbs 13:20 NIV

Relational Prosperity

Individuals and families who are intentional about investing in quality relationships are those who, over time, enjoy the fruit of loving others well. When Charlie and Patty Renfroe, whom I mentioned in chapter 3, faced their greatest time of need, they saw the fruit of their generous love for each other.

Just six years earlier, Rita and I had attended Charlie's seventy-fifth birthday. Like investing money, Charlie and Patty had invested their love and resources in relationships over a lifetime, and the compounding effect of love and admiration was evident in the room that night.

The traffic was snarled on that rainy Friday evening in Atlanta. Already fatigued from a full week of work, why would Rita and I get back into the car and drive ninety minutes bumper to bumper into Buckhead? One compelling reason: The investment one man and his family had made in me and my family over the past thirty years motivated me out of gratitude to honor Charlie on his seventy-fifth birthday. An intimate group of immediate family and close friends gathered to laugh, cry, and affirm the one who brought such richness into our lives.

I watched and reflected as toasts began to flow like a river of delight, bursting forth with refreshing force. A widow wept gracefully: "Charlie, you were the

33 Zig Ziglar, *See You at the Top* (Pelican, 1977), 40.

coast guard for me when Sam died." A grandchild gushed in gratitude: "Pop, you and MeMe were there for me when my mom died. I'll never forget how you cared for me." Four children beamed in admiration and love for a dad who uniquely loved each of them while friends expressed how they felt special because of their relationship with Charlie. I was honored to give a prayer of thanks to God for a life so well spent.

Thank you, Lord, for giving Charlie abundant relational riches.

Solomon reminded us of the value of relationships in Ecclesiastes: "Two are better than one, because they have a good return for their labor: If either of them falls down, one can help the other up" (4:9–10 NIV). Relational prosperity cannot be bought, only sought, by being to others the type of person we want others to be to us, a person who first looks to give, not get; to listen, not talk; to serve, not be served.

We realize the riches of relational wealth as we realize how valuable people are, created in the image of God for the purposes of God. When we value people, we treat them with respect and love them how they need to be loved. Showing respect and love can be as simple as being on time for a meeting or as creative as collecting shared memories in a photo album.

The relationally prosperous are able to see others as the Lord sees them—with great potential to grow into who they are meant to be. A person's stock may be out of favor, but when they are down, they need someone to believe in them and offer future hope beyond their fears. When we buy stock in a person who is at their lowest of lows, we have more potential to one day celebrate with that person. We refresh others as we help restore them back to God's original intent for their lives. How fulfilling to see a friend back in good graces with Christ and living a life that is truly life.

The Power of Generosity: The relationally prosperous are able to see others as the Lord sees them—with great potential to grow into who he wants them to be.

Quality of Life

What does it mean to have quality of life? Good health? Harmony at home? A happy heart? Financial security? Freedom of speech and worship? A fulfilling career? Grateful and content children? A meaningful marriage? A life of significance? Peace with God? Probably some of these elements and more make up a life worth living—a quality life. But the quality of our lives is determined by the quality of our relationships.

Who we spend time with is who we become. If we spend time with those who are wise in their finances and pay attention to their wise way of living, we can learn how to become wise in our own finances. If we worship and pray with those of great faith, we will be intentional in our faith. Our lives reflect our relationships.

How is your relational portfolio? Are you diversified with people who bring value to all aspects of your life? Conversely, are you intentional about investing time and interest in those who look to you for guidance? Quality of life flows not from just receiving wisdom but from giving wisdom. Wisdom works in both directions for the good of the relationship.

Furthermore, be careful not to excuse bad behavior because you are trying to relate to questionable company. Draw a line far away from eroding your character's credibility. You can influence others for good without being bad. In some situations, what you don't do defines you more than what you do. Use business trips and vacations to model faithfulness, not foolishness. Stand for what's right when others agree to do what's wrong. "Do not be misled: 'Bad company corrupts good character'" (1 Corinthians 15:33 NIV).

Above all, quality of life results from your relationship with Christ. He is life itself, and everything good in life flows from him. When you grow in your personal relationship with Jesus, he affects the growth of your other relationships. Relationship building in heaven builds relationships on earth. Ultimately, Jesus is the life to model and follow. The resurrected life of Christ gives you the spiritual stamina to experience a quality life.

> Jesus said to her, "I am the resurrection and the life. The one who believes in me will live, even though they die; and whoever lives by believing in me will never die. Do you believe this?"
>
> "Yes, Lord," she replied, "I believe." (John 11:25–27 NIV)

May we say the same so we can increase the quality of our lives and the lives of those around us because of our relationship with Christ.

Prayer: *Heavenly Father, grow the quality of my relationship with Christ so that out of its joyful overflow, I am able to build quality relationships with those around me. Who are the wise people I spend time with? Am I investing in quality relationships? Guide me to discern your ways. In Jesus' name. Amen.*

The Power of Generosity: The quality of our lives is determined by the quality of our relationships.

Connecting Good People

As you walk in obedience to God, you'll discover many ways to generously bless others, especially in the context of relationships. This includes connecting people with others, fostering new relationships. Here's what I wrote about this in *Essential Habits of Relational Leaders*:

> Making introductions is one of the richest forms of relational giving. Entrusting two people I know to each other for the purpose of them getting to know one another is a true gift. My willingness to use my influence to bring people together for the sake of a growing relationship can be a fruitful investment. I am a much richer person today because friends have unselfishly introduced me to their friends over the years. Many times I have gained a new friend who became a messenger of Christ for me. Relational giving is a catalyst for God's will. Jesus works through people.
>
> Paul was open-handed with his loyal friend Epaphroditus: "Therefore I am all the more eager to send [Epaphroditus], so that when you see him again you may be glad and I may have less anxiety. So then, welcome him in the Lord with great joy, and honor people like him, because he almost died for the work of Christ" (Philippians 2:28–30 [NIV]). His love for his brother, coworker, and fellow soldier in the faith did not keep Paul from sharing this stellar servant of the Lord with other saints in need. Though Paul suffered in a Roman prison, he willingly commissioned his trusted friend to serve other friends at a church hundreds of miles away in Philippi. Paul implored those benefiting from Epaphroditus's sacrifice to welcome him in the Lord joyfully. Grateful recipients of relational generosity honor the gift and the giver.
>
> What friend or acquaintance needs an introduction to someone you know? Someone suffering from an emotional or physical illness may need an introduction to a doctor you know who specializes in their area of pain. A friend who is out of work could use your recommendation to a company that you know is hiring. Maybe you need to release a relationship for a season so that your friend can serve the Lord in another part of the world. Relational generosity is

> risky. Things may not work out, and someone may get hurt. But your part is to obey and patiently trust God to work out His will.[34]

My friend David is an example of a generous connector who refreshes others. David called me one day to introduce me to Chris and Teri. They had just sold their business, and in this new season of life, they were excitedly considering their giving and serving options. David recognized the need for this young couple to be surrounded by other generous families who might model for Chris and Teri how to be intentional in their generosity. Rita and I were blessed to serve generous families in the community that we could introduce to our new friends. Like a relay-race runner, David handed the relational baton to us and never looked back. He knew the power of connecting two couples with complementary experiences and expertise. Because of David's generosity over eight years ago, my wife and I now have a deep friendship with this incredibly generous couple, which has grown through traveling, serving on ministry boards, and attending generosity conferences.[35]

Paul concluded his letter to the Philippians by thanking them for sending gifts that their now-mutual friend Epaphroditus delivered: "I have received full payment and have more than enough. I am amply supplied, now that I have received from Epaphroditus the gifts you sent. They are a fragrant offering, an acceptable sacrifice, pleasing to God" (Philippians 4:18 NIV).

The Power of Generosity: Making introductions is one of the richest forms of relational giving.

Refreshing Others

I have not met a generous person who was not prosperous. They have not always been prosperous financially but certainly relationally, emotionally, and spiritually. Giving people tend to be rich in what matters most.

I am reminded of a couple of friends who sponsor individuals and families to attend the Generous Giving Conference. Annually, Jess and Angela invest thousands of dollars in fifty new people whom they know will be touched by the Spirit to grow in their generosity. They find great joy in helping others discover refreshment in generous living. Leaders prosper and are refreshed when they help others do the same.

---

34 Boyd Bailey, *Essential Habits of Relational Leaders: Building a Culture of Trust* (Harvest House Publishers, 2019), 117–18.

35 Bailey, *Essential Habits of Relational Leaders*, 120.

God's economy is counterintuitive to conventional wisdom. Proverbs teaches that a generous person who gives freely is entrusted by God with more while a stingy person who holds on forfeits his opportunity to gain more from the Lord. "One person gives freely, yet gains even more; another withholds unduly, but comes to poverty" (Proverbs 11:24 NIV). God cannot place blessings in the palm of a hand that is balled up into a greedy fist. But he finds great joy in giving to those who allow blessings to pass through their open hands. Generosity produces prosperity and refreshment. As Paul said, "Remember this: Whoever sows sparingly will also reap sparingly, and whoever sows generously will also reap generously" (2 Corinthians 9:6 NIV).

Do you look for opportunities to be generous with your time, money, wisdom, and relationships? Does your generous giving enrich you and empower others to be generous givers? What you give for God's kingdom is a secure investment with an eternal return. Remember those who took the time to teach and mentor you in your professional career, in faith, in marriage, and in parenting. Pray about whom you can walk alongside and help them grow from your mistakes so they can learn what success really looks like. Like a cold glass of homemade lemonade on a summer day, you will refresh others and be refreshed yourself.

Start by investing time in preparing a generosity plan just as you would create a business plan. Budget your time to be with others for intentional mentoring, coaching, or consulting. Your generosity plan may include putting a percentage of your business revenue in your giving fund at the National Christian Foundation, annually increasing your giving from your personal budget by 1 percent, or seeding a giving fund for your children to start practicing the habit of generous giving. Most of all, generously allot time to sit quietly before the Lord and discern his heart for your life of generosity and prayerfully connect generous friends with generous friends.

Prayer: *Lord, give me a generous heart in coaching and connecting others. Help me share wisdom, offer guidance, and build meaningful connections that bring others closer to you. In Jesus' name. Amen.*

The Power of Generosity: Relational people are generous in coaching and connecting other people.

Growing Relationships over a Lifetime

The National Association for Stock Car Auto Racing (NASCAR) has one of the most loyal and rabid fan bases, people who have been deeply influenced by the sport's intoxicating effect. Though I am not a fan, I am amazed by those who are enamored by the sport's entertaining allure. An innovative ministry leader in this industry was in my office last year, and she educated me on how she builds relationships at raceway sporting events, and in the process, she earns the right to share the gospel. What a creative way to go to the people and get to know them so they might come to know Jesus!

Blogger Amy Martin describes the process that NASCAR leaders have used to build their fan base:

- Access leads to connection. (Because all are welcome to experience the racetrack, they become loyal fans.)
- Connection leads to relationships. (Fans then reach out to others who have not experienced racing.)
- Relationships lead to affinity. (Sharing a common experience creates a bond.)
- Affinity leads to influence. (Comradery within the large, diverse NASCAR community inspires people to listen to and trust each other's thoughts.)
- Influence leads to conversion. (These fans would likely buy anything this driver is selling.)[36]

As we learn how to love like Jesus and enjoy access with him, we can share the good news with our everyday relationships and new friends. Here is how we can apply the NASCAR process of developing devoted fans to influence others for Christ.

Access Leads to Connection

Several years ago, I hoped to meet Steve, who led a family foundation in southern Florida. We had a mutual friend who agreed to set up a meeting for us to get to know one another. It turned out that this other friend of mine and I had served our new acquaintance's father several years before at a mountain resort. This shared experience and access to a mutual friend initiated our connection.

36 Amy Jo Martin, "How NASCAR Uses Access to Build the Most Loyal Brand Fans Anywhere," *Fast Company*, October 15, 2012, https://www.fastcompany.com.

When you give people access to your life, interests, and relationships, you grow understanding and trust.

Connection Leads to Relationships

Steve, the third-generation family foundation leader, was passionate about helping faith-based ministries build organizational capacity. He asked thoughtful questions that revealed his interest in our best practices certification for faith-based ministries and his willingness to engage in our yearlong program personally. Over the next twelve months, we were able to build a relationship during our monthly shared experience of teaching, training, and coaching. Growing a relationship takes intentionality.

Relationships are like a tender seedling—they require attention and care. Each person waters with time and cultivates with understanding. Similar to a NASCAR fan inviting an acquaintance to a race for the first time, you can invite someone you would like to know better to an experience you both would enjoy: a sporting event, training seminar, men's or women's conference, concert, church, game of golf, tennis match, hike, or business opportunity. Be willing and generous to invest time and money to grow relational equity. Over time, the relationship takes root and eventually bears fruit. This leads us to the next progression in gaining influence.

Relationships Lead to Affinity

Dedication to a common interest increases the likelihood of two people growing closer by getting to know each other. An excuse to hang out together over a worthwhile project grows affinity.

My new friend Steve and I were both passionate about helping faith-based ministries build organizational capacity so that they could most effectively further their God-given mission and vision. We experimented with an executive leadership group model that proved to be a most valuable collaborative process in which leaders could exchange ideas, resources, and relationships. Steve's foundation generously provided scholarships, and we were able to provide leadership. I knew our affinity had solidified the moment we celebrated our results and discovered ways to improve.

Affinity Leads to Influence

Because I trusted and respected Steve, I was very open to his input on how to improve our best practices training and coaching. I felt the same trust and respect from him. Steve was very interested in our organizational growth plan and the financial and human resources required to advance to the next level. Our shared interests grew our friendship with each other.

Now you might feel like you don't have a year to grow an affinity with another person or organization. You need help now! I truly feel your angst, but part of the shift in learning to love like Jesus is to think about rich relationships in the long term, not the short term. We must trust that God's timing is best for everyone, and we need to guard against using people for our own agenda and having only shallow interest in theirs. Long-term relationships expand influence.

Influence Leads to Conversion

Another way to think about influence leading to conversion is that influence can lead to becoming a raving fan. Because of the generosity and practical wisdom of Steve and his family, our team became raving fans of their passion and priorities as a foundation. Instead of just looking to our interests (which we were compelled to follow), we learned how to appreciate the value of what a third-generation organization like his had to offer. By taking time to learn from them, we were also able to educate them in the ideas that we had developed over the years. Everyone was better for the arrangement and connection. *We* are better than *me*!

Three years into our relationship, Steve casually asked me one day how his foundation could make a significant investment into Ministry Ventures (which, by God's grace, I cofounded with my friend Mike). I explained our vision to repurpose our content for an online learning platform, which resonated with his entrepreneurial DNA. Over the following three years, after improving our plan with the foundation's input, Steve's organization gave a significant six-figure gift to Ministry Ventures to practice what we preached about innovation and growth. The results were stunning, and their gift reaped a harvest tenfold what they invested.

Relational conversion may involve an individual coming to faith because of your influence, or it might mean that an organization enjoys favor from God and people because of your faithfulness to invest for the long term.

The Power of Generosity: The relationally generous pour into others without expecting anything in return.

Influencing Others in Generosity

I met Greg and Jan Winchester at a Journey of Generosity (JOG) gathering. A JOG is a twenty-two-hour interactive small group experience with twelve to fifteen people. We enjoy videos of stories of generous people, Bible discussions on generosity, and individual prayer time to listen to God's heart related to our generosity toward him and others. The Winchesters are passionate followers of Jesus Christ. Early in their marriage, they were impacted by a Dallas, Texas, businessman's teaching on biblical generosity. They became aligned with living a lifestyle of generosity and being intentional with their five children about growing their hearts of generosity. As a family, they prayed about how they could have the most impact on growing God's kingdom.

Because of their passion for Scripture and the world, they prayed for ways to spread the good news of Jesus Christ and his Word to every continent. Over the next twenty years, they built relationships on all seven continents with leaders whom the Lord had called to spread his Word. Each story was unique and fascinating, with the most recent being their support of the restoration of the Winchester Bible in England (possibly a distant family connection). The entire family was able to visit and experience the restoration process of a centuries-old Bible. Greg recalled that he nervously held the sacred Scripture, afraid that he might drop and damage it.

In Atlanta, Georgia, the Winchesters served as giving champions. They hosted conversations about generosity in their home so that up to thirty people could collaboratively learn from others' ideas for generous living. This three-hour gathering over dinner and rich discussions expanded our generous community. In these heartfelt exchanges, young, emerging givers begin to understand that generosity is not just about money but about a way of living and sharing time, resources, and care. As they experience the beauty of giving, they're encouraged to invest more deeply in the needs around them, creating a ripple effect of generosity that strengthens and blesses the entire community. In addition, Greg and Jan made available their two vacation homes for destination JOGs. Our young, emerging givers loved this adventurous opportunity!

Greg also leveraged his influence at church to take some key leaders through the JOG experience. Greg, Jan, and their adult children are generosity champions who use their influence and resources to create environments for the Lord to raise up generous disciples of Jesus Christ.[37]

37 To learn more about Journey of Generosity, visit https://generousgiving.org/events/jog.

The Power of Generosity: Your influence and resources are impactful in helping others on their generosity journey.

Generosity Helps Heal Injustice

My friend Durwood Snead called a few years ago, burdened to do something after reading the book *Blood at the Root* by Patrick Phillips. This heartbreaking story outlines the cruel injustices of early twentieth-century racism in Forsyth County, Georgia.

After an eighteen-year-old White woman was raped and killed, one Black man was lynched, and two other Black teens were arrested, quickly convicted, and hanged for the crime. Angry mobs terrorized the community of Black residents with an ultimatum to relocate out of the county immediately or face the destruction of their property or even death. Overnight, 1,098 Black people made their way out of Forsyth County to a safe area to start over.[38] This gut-wrenching, horrific story broke Durwood's heart. As he prayed, he felt the Lord lead him to bless the descendants of the displaced families by setting up a college scholarship fund.

He opened a donor-advised fund with the National Christian Foundation to receive gifts for the scholarships. Durwood wisely met with Black pastors in the area to gain their approval and feedback. A local, influential church became an avid promoter of the scholarship fund. In addition, some of our NCF families are passionate about correcting past injustices and being able to educate others as an expression of Jesus Christ's love. They supported this cause through their generous gifts to the scholarship fund, and many of them attended the celebration service at the church in support of these upcoming college freshmen.

In the first year, God blessed Durwood's fund with $66,000 awarded toward nine scholarships.[39] An application process was implemented to vet the candidates. Once the scholarship recipients were chosen, the celebration service was scheduled at the church. Some of our friends who attended the celebration were moved to tears because of how the power of generosity helped heal relationships and gave tangible hope and resources to love people practically. The thank-you letters written by the students were priceless.

Here are some excerpts from thank-you letters three of the students sent Durwood and the generous givers who provided the college scholarships:

38 Patrick Phillips, *Blood at the Root: A Racial Cleansing in America* (W. W. Norton, 2016).
39 Sheila Dolinger, "Future of Hope: Scholarship Honors Black Descendants of Racial Injustice," National Christian Foundation, February 20, 2023, https://www.ncfgiving.com.

- "This scholarship has allowed me more freedom to focus on my academics than having to focus on everything else life has to throw at me. Thank you for the assistance that you all bring. It makes me so happy to know that someone cares and is willing to help."
- "I am profoundly grateful to the scholarship team for not only recognizing the impact of historical adversity on my family but also providing us with the transformative opportunity to build a brighter future through education."
- "I express heartfelt gratitude to the generous donors for their invaluable contribution to the scholarship. Their support has significantly eased the financial burden on my family, opening doors to educational opportunities that will have a lasting impact on our lives. Thank you for making a meaningful difference in our journey."

Durwood and a few generous givers are making a difference by being Jesus in a very tangible, unifying manner. By God's grace, healing relationships have elevated the quality of life in our community for God's glory.

The Power of Generosity: Generosity can bring relational healing when given in Jesus' name.

Focus on Generously Loving God

"Love the LORD your God, listen to his voice, and hold fast to him. For the LORD is your life" (Deuteronomy 30:20 NIV). The Christian life is a matter of focus. Do I focus on my fears, my problems, and my needs, or do I focus on God? Do I love him, listen to him, trust him, and allow him to consume my life, or am I wrapped up in myself? These are two very different perspectives. One takes life; the other gives life. One saps energy; the other gives energy. So how can we listen to God, trust God, and make God our life? It starts with love.

When we love God, our affections are heavenward. "Since, then, you have been raised with Christ, set your hearts on things above, where Christ is, seated at the right hand of God. Set your minds on things above, not on earthly things" (Colossians 3:1–2 NIV). Love means we want to be with him, understand him, and please him. Loving God means our love for others or things pales in comparison to our love for him.

Others may become jealous because of the time and attention you give God. It may be hard for them to understand, but in reality, if your love of God is pure, those closest to you will be better off. Because the Lord loves you and you love him, you cannot help but love those around you. "This is how we know what love is: Jesus Christ laid down his life for us. And we ought to lay down our lives for our brothers and sisters" (1 John 3:16 NIV).

Focusing on God also means you listen to him. Quietness and solitude become a part of who you are because God's voice is clear and crisp during stillness and reflection. Other competing noises are snuffed out when you take time to listen. Listen to him in contemplative worship music, listen to him through meditation on his Word, or listen to him beside a bubbling brook under the canopy of his creation. His voice is constant and soothing. He is everywhere, searching to communicate with and comfort his children.

How well do you listen to the Lord? Does it take a posture of desperation? Do the ears of your soul perk up in the presence of your holy Creator? How can we not listen to the one who holds the world in his hands and who loves us beyond comprehension? Indeed, listen to him and quickly do what he says. Obedience acts on what it hears by faith.

Trust is also a part of our focus on God. We can trust him because he is trustworthy. Others will let us down, but God won't. He is always there to comfort us in our affliction and to convict us of our sins. Trust his flawless character. Out of this trust flows peace that this life does not offer. Trust most especially during uncertain times, for he will work it out for his glory. Relational riches start with our rich time with the Lord. "The LORD's unfailing love surrounds the one who trusts in him" (Psalm 32:10 NIV).

Prayer: *Lord, your generous love draws me closer, compelling me to spend time with you. Fill me with a longing to know you deeply and dwell in your presence daily. In Jesus' name. Amen.*

The Power of Generosity: Your generous love of God compels you to spend generous time with God.

Summary of "Being Relationally Intentional"

- The relationally prosperous are able to see others as the Lord sees them—with great potential to grow into who he wants them to be.
- The quality of our lives is determined by the quality of our relationships.
- Making introductions is one of the richest forms of relational giving.
- Relational people are generous in coaching and connecting other people.
- The relationally generous pour into others without expecting anything in return.
- Your influence and resources are impactful in helping others on their generosity journey.
- Generosity can bring relational healing when given in Jesus' name.
- Your generous love of God compels you to spend generous time with God.

A Generous Prayer

Heavenly Father, teach me the beauty of relational generosity. Help me to extend kindness without expectation and to give freely of my time, attention, and resources. May my interactions be marked by empathy, understanding, and selflessness to mirror your boundless love for me. Guide me to see the needs of others as opportunities to share your blessings, to foster deeper connections, and to strengthen bonds of friendship and community. Grant me the grace to forgive as you forgive me and to love extravagantly as you love me. In practicing relational generosity, may I reflect our generous relationship and bring glory to your name. Amen.

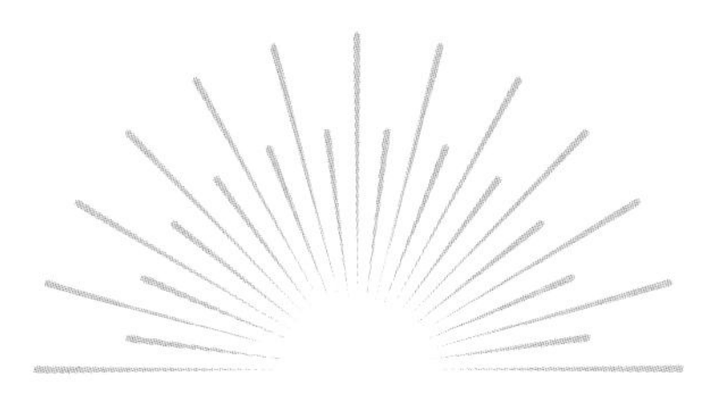

CHAPTER 7

Serving Humbly

You are rewarded not according to time or work
but according to the measure of your love.
Catherine of Siena

You have been called to live in freedom, my brothers and sisters.
But don't use your freedom to satisfy your sinful nature.
Instead, use your freedom to serve one another in love.
Galatians 5:13 NLT

The Fruit of Humility

The fruit of humility is generous service to others. Think about those whom you know who are humble of heart, not looking to be the center of attention but looking to help others. When you reflect on these other-centered friends, aren't you attracted to the almost effortless manner in which they celebrate God's blessings with gratitude and how they express their gratefulness by seeking to be a blessing to others? It can be so refreshing and attractive! Such are the generous expressions of a humble, grateful life.

A close look at the lifestyle of Jesus reveals his manner of intentionally showing the way to those who were lost, confused, and neglected. Jesus gave glory and gratitude to his Father and, out of this humble attitude, sought to serve and love others so they might give glory and gratitude to God.

Paul called for humility in Ephesians 4:1–2: "Walk in a manner worthy of the calling…with all humility and gentleness, with patience, bearing with one another in love" (ESV). A humble heart is the foyer of a life that flows into other inviting rooms of gentleness, patience, and love. This passage could be a commentary on the opening words of Jesus' famous teaching in Matthew 5:3: "Blessed are the poor in spirit: for theirs is the kingdom of heaven" (KJV).

Humility is the first step to a generous life. It serves as the foundation to build on as we seek to apply our Lord's more challenging teachings of turning the other cheek, praying for and loving our enemies, and defending the sanctity of marriage, to name a few. Without the foundation of humility, Jesus' beatitudes, which are statements of blessing, can feel burdensome and unachievable. But lived out with a spirit of humility, they are life-changing and compelling arguments for generous living through the power of Jesus Christ.

Alexander Maclaren beautifully elevated the essential nature of being poor in spirit, the first and foundational beatitude in the Sermon on the Mount:

> To be poor in spirit is to be in inmost reality conscious of need, of emptiness, of dependence on God, of demerit; the true estimate of self, as blind, evil, weak, is intended; the characteristic tone of feeling pointed to is self-abnegation.... Christ begins His portraiture of a citizen of the kingdom with the consciousness of want and sin. All the rest of the morality of the Sermon is founded on this. It is the root of all that is heavenly and divine in character. So this teaching is dead against the modern pagan doctrine of self-reliance, and really embodies the very principle for the supposed omission of which some folk like this Sermon; namely, that our proud self-confidence must be broken down before God can do any good with us, or we can enter His kingdom.[40]

Humility first gives 100 percent to God and then looks to serve for God. I read this moving story recently describing a generous, humble, and gentle soul:

> One hot afternoon on a beach, people noticed a young girl drowning. They quickly rescued her. The little girl was unconscious. An old man from a nearby cottage hurriedly reached for the girl laid down on the seashore. As the old man was about to hold the girl, a furious guy warned the people surrounding the girl to step aside, including the old man.
>
> "I was trained to do CPR. Stay out of this! Let me do it!" the guy exclaimed.
>
> The old man stood up and stepped behind the guy and watched quietly while the latter was performing CPR for the girl.

40 Alexander Maclaren, "The New Sinai," in *Expositions of Holy Scripture: St. Matthew Chapters 1 to 8* (S. S. Scranton, 1900), 99–100.

> After almost a minute, the little girl regained consciousness. The people around them felt relieved and began applauding the guy. The old man, who looked very happy, gratefully congratulated the guy as well.
>
> After two hours, however, the guy who saved the girl suddenly felt too much fatigue, experienced difficulty in breathing and became unconscious. A few minutes later, he woke up in an ambulance rushing him to the nearest hospital. Beside him was the old man he saw earlier at the beach now checking his pulse rate. The old man did CPR on him while he was unconscious. This time he learned that the old man was a doctor.
>
> "Why didn't you tell me you're a doctor?" he asked.
>
> The doctor just smiled and answered: "It doesn't matter to me whether you call me a doctor or not. A precious life was in danger. I became a doctor, not for fame, but to save lives. We had the same goal, and that was to save the girl. Nothing can surpass the feeling that you have just saved another life. There's a lot of things to be protected other than our ego."[41]

Yes, we all grow in humility when we are gentle and patient, bearing with one another in love.

Prayer: *Heavenly Father, give me a generous heart of humility to live and patiently bear with others in love through Christ's love and in Jesus' name. Amen.*

The Power of Generosity: A humble heart generously serves others.

Love Serves in Humility

Soldiers in Christ's army enlist to serve others. They serve at their Savior's pleasure and unselfishly serve fellow servants of the Lord. Servants of Jesus are first responders to the needs that afflict or attack the body of Christ. There is no waiting to be drafted because salvation in Jesus assumes service. Like apple pie is just part of America, generous love and serving others is an extension of being a Christian, a platform for humility, and an expression of Jesus.

Love is the motivation for Christ-centered service. We volunteer at church, assist in the parking lot, serve in the nursery, or lead a small group because we love. We clean up the kitchen after a meal because we love. We manage the home finances, wash clothes, cook, do yard work, help a child with homework, visit a

41 "A Story of Real Humility," Grow and Teach, July 29, 2016, https://growteach.wordpress.com.

sick friend, give a gift, and write a caring note because we love. Love cannot *not* serve. Our service says, *I love you.*

"Each of you should use whatever gift you have received to serve others, as faithful stewards of God's grace in its various forms" (1 Peter 4:10 NIV). Service to others is a generous deed of gratitude to God. He has blessed you with stuff for your use to serve others. He gave you a house to host guests and to take in those who need a place to stay. He gave you a car to provide transportation for those who need a ride to work, the grocery store, school, or just away. He gave you time to invest in others: their children, their spiritual lives, their financial needs, their health, or their emotional wellness.

Your generous service also benefits you. You feel fulfilled having filled up another's emotional cup with healthy feelings. Your faith grows when you take the time to build up another's belief in God. You are more accountable when you teach others the commands of Christ. You are a candidate for service from others as they seek to show gratitude to God and to you. You serve not to benefit or be served, but this is the outcome of loving Christ. Serve others for Christ's sake and watch him work. You serve Jesus by serving others. "This, then, is how you ought to regard us: as servants of Christ and as those entrusted with the mysteries God has revealed. Now it is required that those who have been given a trust must prove faithful" (1 Corinthians 4:1–2 NIV).

Prayer: *Heavenly Father, whom can I serve for you with my time, talents, and treasure? Where are you leading me to love and serve in this season of my life? I ask you to lead me through Christ's love and in Jesus' name. Amen.*

The Power of Generosity: Servants of Jesus are first responders when forces afflict or attack the body of Christ.

What Breaks Your Heart?

Our pastor recently asked us this revealing question during his Sunday morning sermon. He went on to emphasize that when you find what breaks your heart, you need to do something about it. My wife and I processed this probing question over lunch after church. Rita prefers time to process questions and ideas, but the Lord had made it clear to her that children at risk are what breaks her heart. Soon after, in sync with the Holy Spirit's work in Rita's heart, she was asked to serve on the board of a local ministry, Saving Susan.

Tracy and Jay Arntzen founded this ministry in 2014 to partner with and support Christian homes and orphanages in developing countries so that children can have food, clothing, shelter, and education. This ministry is a gift for these precious children, providing protection from and preventing human trafficking. Here is how their ministry website describes Jay's initial visit to Cambodia:

> Jay Arntzen, along with his middle son Jared, joined a team from Sanctuary Church on a mission trip to Cambodia.
>
> At Bileg Solid Rock children's home, Jay met a young orphaned girl named Vichika. Exhausted by the long flights and time change, Jay couldn't pronounce her name and called her "Susan." Jay and Susan bonded instantly and he wanted to adopt her, but he learned that Cambodia's borders were closed to adoption.[42]

After a full year of prayer, Jay and Tracy launched a parent-partner idea. Parent Partners became the core strategy of the Saving Susan Ministry. Parent Partners regularly video chat with a child, pray for them, help them financially, and make at least one in-person visit. Their relationship continues until the child completes college and launches into the workforce. Today fifty-seven children are in a supportive Parent Partner relationship.

I have watched Rita generously love children for most of our lives, so I am not surprised to watch her flourish in her role on the board of Saving Susan. She recently traveled to Cambodia and was overwhelmed by the needs and equally excited about the joy in the lives of these children who love the Lord and are hopeful in his love.

Take some time to ponder and pray about what breaks your heart. This is often God's way of showing you how you can humbly serve his creation.

Generous Prayers and Provision

Tracy and Jay believe the Lord led them to formally organize Saving Susan in 2014. The ministry was birthed in prayer, and it has been sustained by prayer ever since. The board gathers once a month in person or by Zoom to pray for the ministry, the children, and the Parent Partners. God's favor is on the ministry because its leadership understands and embraces Psalm 127:1: "Unless the Lord builds the house, the builders labor in vain" (NIV).

The financial model of Saving Susan is also compelling. Jay and Tracy's elevator manufacturing company, along with a few generous givers, funds the

42 "Our Story," Saving Susan Ministry, accessed June 26, 2024, https://www.savingsusanministry.org.

operational costs of the ministry. So 100 percent of the donations the program receives directly reach the children.[43] Jay and Tracy give because of God's generosity in their lives. They are also compelled to give because of the needs of these children and Christ's love for them. Such is his kingdom. God's heart breaks, their heart breaks, and what breaks our hearts can make us more like Jesus. And, by God's grace, the hearts of children are being healed, and souls are being saved.

What breaks your heart is often a sign of what God has called you to help heal or change. When you feel a deep, compassionate ache for something—whether it's injustice, suffering, or the lost—it's an invitation from God to step in and make a difference. Here are three practical ways to respond:

1. **Pray for Guidance:** Ask God to reveal how he wants you to act. Pray for the people, situation, or cause that weighs on your heart.
2. **Take Small Steps:** Start with simple acts of kindness or service. Volunteer, donate, or support someone in need.
3. **Build Awareness:** Share your passion with others, inspiring them to care. By raising awareness, you create a ripple effect, inviting others to join in God's work.

Once you have identified something that breaks your heart, commit to prayer. Seek the Lord to discover how he would like to use you to serve to alleviate this hurt in the world. Embrace what breaks your heart as God's invitation to make a meaningful impact.

Prayer: *Lord, reveal to me what breaks my heart and help me respond with compassion. Guide me to act with courage and love so that I can make a difference where you lead. In Jesus' name. Amen.*

The Power of Generosity: Activate generosity toward what breaks your heart to bring the love of Jesus Christ to save and heal.

Humble Service for the Vulnerable

Wilson Lee was born not too long ago. He is our baby daughter's first baby—joy unspeakable! Five days after Wilson's birth, I asked my son-in-law Tyler what he thought about his son, swaddled and sweet.

"Boyd, he poops, pees, eats, sleeps, and is high-maintenance, but I love him so much!" He went on: "My deep love for Wilson reminds me of how much God loves me—in spite of my messy condition."

43 "Core Values," Saving Susan Ministry, accessed August 7, 2024, https://www.savingsusanministry.org.

Here is a twenty-eight-year-old who truly understands and enjoys the Lord's lavish love. My heavenly Father loves me in my mess and stress so that I can welcome, care for, generously love, and serve others.

Jesus illustrated to his ambitious disciples the need to deflate their egos and inflate their humble hearts. "Anyone who humbles himself as this little child is the greatest in the Kingdom of Heaven. And any of you who welcomes a little child like this because you are mine is welcoming me and caring for me" (Matthew 18:4–5 TLB). Greatness, to God, is a childlike vulnerability that gladly acknowledges a deep dependence on the Lord—a neediness only the comfort and guidance of the Holy Spirit can fulfill. Furthermore, born from our childlike faith is thoughtful and intentional love toward little ones. Love welcomes and cares for children as if we were caring for Christ. Service flows from a humble heart.

Serving and caring for the vulnerable are calls to embody Christ's compassion. We can begin by offering our time, whether by visiting the elderly, supporting struggling families, or listening to those in pain. Practical help—like providing meals, donating clothing, or assisting with transportation—meets immediate needs and shows tangible love. Advocacy, using our voices to support policies and causes that protect and uplift vulnerable groups, is another powerful way to care. Finally, prayer is essential; praying for wisdom, protection, and comfort over those in need reminds us that God's strength is ultimately what sustains and heals. Through these actions, we reflect God's generous heart.

Children are one of Christ's greatest reminders of what he expects in our relationship with him. Like a child, we approach our heavenly Father with honesty about our fears, humility about our sins, and loving trust in our hearts. And be encouraged, for your sacrifice and service for your children are sacrifices and services for your Savior. When you welcome their concerns and care for their hearts, you welcome and care for Christ. Don't stay stressed in your mess. Rather, in humility, let God lift you by his love for generous service to his kingdom.

Jesus reminded us that serving the vulnerable is serving Jesus: "Truly I tell you, whatever you did for one of the least of these brothers and sisters of mine, you did for me" (Matthew 25:40 NIV).

Prayer: *Heavenly Father, grow my heart of humility and love toward you and with others. In Jesus' name. Amen.*

The Power of Generosity: Love welcomes and cares for others as if you were serving Jesus Christ.

Faith-Driven Work

Paul used his work to help spread the gospel. "Paul went to see [Pricilla and Aquila], and because he was a tentmaker as they were, he stayed and worked with them. Every Sabbath he reasoned in the synagogue, trying to persuade Jews and Greeks" (Acts 18:2–4 NIV).

Business is an everyday opportunity to be an excellent example of a Jesus follower. It is a professional platform to perform good deeds and exhibit integrity in business interactions. The sacred and secular are partners in business, for a kingdom mission models actions that speak louder than words. When the quality of work exceeds the industry standard, people begin to ask why. Indeed, a company that acknowledges Christ as the owner is positioned for God's favor.

Do the values of your company mirror the heart of Jesus? Do you embrace honesty, humility, and hard work as everyday virtues to live out? Are team members quick to serve, find solutions, and give positive feedback? If our work culture reflects the character of Christ, we will attract team members with the character, competency, and chemistry to take the company to the next level. Great people are not motivated by money alone but by a mission much greater than themselves. Greatness comes to a company that has a greater purpose. "You yourselves are our letter, written on our hearts, known and read by everyone. You show that you are a letter from Christ, the result of our ministry, written not with ink but with the Spirit of the living God, not on tablets of stone but on tablets of human hearts" (2 Corinthians 3:2–3 NIV).

Is your real mission just to make money, or is it to transform lives? Is the creed of your culture going the second mile in service to the customer, or do you see your customers merely as a means to a financial end? An enterprise that glorifies God with outstanding service and superior products will produce fruit that remains. Become better, and you will become bigger for the right reasons. Your work done well is a testament to God's grace, faithfulness, and favor.

Furthermore, a leader who submits to the Lord does not lord their faith over other team members. A humble leader's heart is governed by gratitude so that they lead and manage out of appreciation and accountability, not as an intimidating, autocratic ruler. Even if a supervisor or employee does not believe in Jesus, they can still behave like Jesus. When we create a culture friendly to faith, we grow a team of people who have faith in each other.

Therefore, intentionally integrate scriptural principles into your life and work. Use your business or ministry to make life better for people and people better for life. Be bold to tastefully and professionally pray for people. Give time off for team members to invest in their marriages and travel on mission trips. Grow leaders who will pour into their teams. Dedicate your company to Christ, and he will determine your steps for success.

Prayer: *Heavenly Father, I dedicate the company I work for to you for your purposes. In Jesus' name. Amen.*

The Power of Generosity: Your work is your ministry to generously love others in Jesus' name.

A Generous Business on Mission

Beautifully and strategically, the Lord has led our friends Clayton and Emily Edwards, third-generation entrepreneurs, to use their apartment business to bless their tenants. They have been able to humbly serve the many lives impacted by their company. My colleagues at the National Christian Foundation and Clayton and Emily gave me permission to share their story.

As the third-generation owner and operator of Kenco Residential, Clayton's journey into redemptive real estate began decades ago and is marked by many mentors who stepped in to guide him along the way.

Ken Edwards, Clayton's grandfather, started Kenco Residential in the 1960s. By the time Clayton was born, Kenco Residential was a thriving, family-run property management company with a handful of apartment complexes that Grandpa Ken had built himself in the Atlanta area.

Clayton's father continued this legacy, teaching Clayton how to earn money, steward possessions, work hard, and be generous. His father said, "God created the world, God created us, and God created money. It's all God's. You use your gifts and skills. You work hard. You make money, and then you give the first part of it back to God."[44] Clayton applied his father's lessons from his preschool household chores to his preteen lawn-care business and beyond.

Yet when Clayton was young, the family's business mission confused him. It read, "Glorify God, and treat others the way we would want to be treated."

Clayton went to his father and said, "You're in the property management business. What does this mission have to do with apartments?"

His father replied, "You're missing it. This is all God's."[45]

44 Lauren Street, "Clayton Edwards: Property Management with a Purpose," National Christian Foundation, July 14, 2024, https://www.ncfgiving.com.
45 Street, "Clayton Edwards."

When Clayton joined his family's company, he focused on providing affordable, safe homes for those living in the Atlanta area who made between $40,000 and $70,000 a year. He accumulated older apartment communities in good locations, and Kenco Residential grew exponentially. "Clayton's 'first fruits' went from $10,000 to $100,000 to $1 million, and he found himself unsure how to best steward the resources God had entrusted to him. Should he give it all to his church? Should he invest it?"[46]

When Clayton and I met at NCF Georgia, we came up with a plan for Clayton's giving. Clayton began considering questions like, *What are my values? What Bible verses resonate most with me? What do I want people to say at my funeral?* I also introduced Clayton to the idea of three P's, which are the key to generosity and stewardship:

- **Priority:** Give to God the firstfruits, the first portion of your income, before saving and even before paying your bills.
- **Percentage:** Give a predetermined percentage of your gross income.
- **Progression:** Increase the percentage of your giving over time. Whether it's going from 1 percent to 2 percent or 10 percent to 100 percent, what's important is that the percentage is growing.

Even as he started giving to church and missionaries, he sensed God was calling him to something more. He could hear God saying, "You've got 20 employees. Do they know you're a believer? Are they believers? What about these apartment communities? You own the property, and you don't even know your people. You don't know who lives there, what they are like, and what their needs are."[47]

Then the 2020 pandemic began, and the needs of his employees and residents became apparent. He began to see apartments as places where people could experience purpose, connection, and God's love. Using the funds God was calling him to set aside from Kenco Residential's profits, Clayton envisioned offering on-site support for his residents through therapists, social workers, childcare providers, and community engagement specialists. From this vision came Atlanta Connected Communities, a separate nonprofit business located within Clayton's apartment complexes.

46 Street, "Clayton Edwards."
47 Street, "Clayton Edwards."

Knowing he would need help bringing his vision for Atlanta Connected Communities to life, Clayton recruited Stephanie Johnston, a social worker who had just returned to the US from serving as a missionary in Spain. Stephanie talked to many of the residents of Clayton's complexes to identify three of their most common needs: mental health, financial needs, and logistical needs. People longed for social camaraderie, were tired of living paycheck to paycheck, and needed practical advice or assistance to provide for their daily needs like childcare and transportation. These are the needs Clayton strives to meet through Atlanta Connected Communities. He and his team even host a monthly dinner so residents can share a homemade meal together.

When residents ask Clayton why he's helping them, he's ready with an answer: "We're helping you because we believe that what unites us is greater than what divides us. I'm sharing with you what's in my heart, which is Jesus. It's God's love."[48] When they hear his response, they want to know more about this God whom Clayton thinks is so important. And that, Clayton says, is the driving force behind Atlanta Connected Communities. He sees each property as an opportunity to plant little churches.

But he's not finished. As Atlanta Connected Communities integrates into every Kenco property, Clayton is dreaming for how he can grow his funding and the nonprofit's influence, hopefully encouraging other Christian real estate owners to start similar programs across the country.

Prayer: *Lord, help me lead with generosity in my work. May it be a platform for good. Use its influence to uplift and better the lives of all it touches. In Jesus' name. Amen.*

The Power of Generosity: A generous business uses its influence to better the lives that it impacts.

Serve with Gladness

My energy level to serve ebbs and flows, but one thing is for sure: My motivation to help others comes alive when my service is focused on the Lord with a glad and grateful heart. "Serve the Lord with gladness," Psalm 100:2 says (KJV). I am glad and grateful to be alive, glad and grateful to be a beloved child of God, and glad and grateful for family, friends, and a faith community. Like a daily spiritual vitamin, gratitude and gladness fill a soul's deficiencies. Our gladness in service is an outflow of abiding in the joy of the Lord. It is not merely a duty but a divine

48 Street, "Clayton Edwards."

calling that permeates every facet of our lives. Scripture underscores the significance of serving with joy, reminding us of the immeasurable blessings that flow from a heart devoted to service. This encompasses serving in the church, in the community, and within the family—a threefold tapestry that weaves together the essence of our devotion to God.

Within the fellowship of the church, our service becomes an expression of reverence and gratitude to the Lord. Ephesians 4:11–12 reminds us that God has equipped each of us uniquely for service within his body, the church. Whether through teaching, music, administration, or acts of kindness, every contribution is an opportunity to extend God's love and grace to those within the congregation. The joy of serving in the church emanates from the unity of purpose, the fellowship of believers, and the shared commitment to glorify God through our collective efforts.

Beyond the church walls, our service extends to the broader community. Jesus himself exemplified this when he washed his disciples' feet, teaching us that true greatness lies in humble service (John 13:1–17). Engaging in outreach programs, volunteering in shelters, or simply extending a helping hand to those in need mirrors Christ's compassionate heart. Serving our community reflects the love of Christ. Our actions reveal his presence and bring hope to a world longing for compassion and care.

Within the confines of our homes, serving our families becomes a sacred duty. Ephesians 6:4 instructs fathers to nurture and guide their children in the Lord's ways, emphasizing the family's pivotal role in spiritual upbringing. And Proverbs 31:27–28 celebrates the diligent and nurturing care a mother provides, honoring her commitment to her family and the blessings that flow from her dedication: "She watches over the affairs of her household and does not eat the bread of idleness. Her children arise and call her blessed; her husband also, and he praises her" (NIV).

Serving our families entails sacrificial love, selflessness, and a commitment to fostering an environment of love, respect, and encouragement. Through acts of service within our households, we mirror God's unconditional love and model the character of Christ, cultivating an atmosphere where each member feels cherished and valued.

Serving with gladness is not a burdensome obligation but a privilege the Lord bestows on us. It is a response to God's immeasurable grace poured out on us. The joy we find in serving is not contingent on circumstances but is rooted in our relationship with Christ. Scripture reminds us that whatever we do, whether in the church, in the community, or within our families, we should do wholeheartedly as unto the Lord, for it is from him that we ultimately receive our reward. "Whatever you do, work heartily, as for the Lord and not for men, knowing that from the Lord you will receive the inheritance as your reward. You are serving the Lord Christ" (Colossians 3:23–24 ESV). Humble service with a glad heart is the fruit of generous living.

Prayer: *Heavenly Father, with a glad and grateful heart, I praise and adore you through Christ's love and in Jesus' name. Amen.*

The Power of Generosity: Humble service with a glad heart is the fruit of generous living.

Summary of "Serving Humbly"

- A humble heart generously serves others.
- Servants of Jesus are first responders when forces afflict or attack the body of Christ.
- Activate generosity toward what breaks your heart to bring the love of Jesus Christ to save and heal.
- Love welcomes and cares for others as if you were serving Jesus Christ.
- Your work is your ministry to generously love others in Jesus' name.
- A generous business uses its influence to better the lives that it impacts.
- Humble service with a glad heart is the fruit of generous living.

A Generous Prayer

Lord, help me embody humble service, as Christ did, by putting others before myself. Teach me to serve with a heart full of love and compassion and to see your image in every person I encounter. May my actions reflect your grace and humility, bringing glory to your name. In serving others, may I find true fulfillment and joy, knowing that in humble service, I am serving Jesus Christ as I am serving others. Amen.

CHAPTER 8

Living Generously

God has a way of giving by the cartloads
to those who give away by shovelfuls.
Charles Spurgeon

A generous person will prosper;
whoever refreshes others will be refreshed.
Proverbs 11:25 NIV

Generosity Prospers and Refreshes

Proverbs clearly says that a generous life is a prosperous life, starting with a soul's prosperity. The word *refresh* implies watering; the waters of heaven generously hydrate and irrigate a prosperous soul with the goal of refreshing another thirsty soul. Charles Spurgeon used watering imagery to depict refreshing others: "My dear brother, you may be a man of talent, you may be a man of wealth: just turn on the big tap, and let your ignorant or poor neighbours benefit a little by your abundance; pull up the flood-gates, and let the more needy brethren be enriched by your fulness: open that mouth of yours that your wisdom may feed many; tell of what God has done for your soul that the humble may hear thereof and be glad."[49]

To give away is the wisest way to live, prosper, and refresh. My friend Clayton and his wife, Emily, whom I mentioned in the last chapter, have shared with me their purpose statement for generous living: "We strive to maximize our gifts, opportunities, and relationships to further God's kingdom as we raise three amazing children and love each other unconditionally. We are faithful stewards

49 Charles Haddon Spurgeon, "The Waterer Watered," The Spurgeon Center for Biblical Preaching at Midwestern Seminary, sermon given April 23, 1865, https://www.spurgeon.org.

of our time, talent, and treasure. We create fertile ground for the gospel and encourage others in Christ as we serve our family, friends, and community."

What I have learned from Clayton, Emily, and others is that to give away is the wisest way to live. It is wise because generosity refreshes and prospers—prospering us with the true riches of relational health with the Lord and people. Generosity grows your trustworthiness with God so you can be trusted with his blessings, and in the process, generosity refreshes you and those you love. "Each of you should use whatever gift you have received to serve others, as faithful stewards of God's grace in its various forms" (1 Peter 4:10 NIV).

To give away is the wisest way to live. Why is it wise to be generous? One reason to be generous is to experience it as a loving form of accountability that protects us from ourselves. Our time, influence, and affluence require intentionality so that they serve God's purposes and are not squandered on self-indulgence. One friend (who invited me to stay at his vacation home to write) uses his influence at work to help employees pay down debt…and he is a banker! Not surprisingly, as his employees prosper from debt-free living, the bank prospers by retaining grateful and great team members. Another friend just transitioned from a forty-year career in corporate culture, and as he says, he is not retiring, just repurposing. After much prayer with his wife, they decided on a time allocation for his repurposing plan: a third of his time for family, a third of his time for mentoring, and a third for himself. Ah yes, intentional, generous living prospers and refreshes.

The Power of Generosity: Fear and doubt take flight when, as God's beloved children, we stay faithful in our generosity and trust him for his very best.

A Charitable Checking Account

There are many ways we can practically practice generous living through our finances. A donor-advised fund (DAF) is like a charitable checking account.[50] At the National Christian Foundation, opening a DAF is free with no minimum amount required. You serve in the donor role and advise NCF which approved 501(c)(3) nonprofit to grant your gift. There is a minimum grant amount to an approved charity of one hundred dollars. So, to clarify, no minimum balance is required to open a fund, but when funds are sent out in the form of a grant, there is a one-hundred-dollar minimum.

50 "Donor-Advised Funds at the National Christian Foundation," National Christian Foundation, accessed August 6, 2024, https://www.ncfgiving.com.

Since 1982, the National Christian Foundation's mission has been to mobilize resources through biblical generosity with a vision to reach and restore every person through the love of Christ. Thousands of families have donor-advised funds with NCF, supporting ninety thousand approved charities that, since the beginning of NCF until 2024, have received grants totaling $20 billion.[51] The donor-advised fund is a resource for people to systematically plan their giving, become more tax efficient, and accelerate their generosity. Generational-minded families open a DAF for their children to help promote a legacy of generosity and offer a seamless succession plan for giving. Families who give together often have aligned values and less conflict over money.

A donor-advised fund is also a vehicle to receive noncash gifts such as public and private stock, real estate, and business interests. Let's explore the benefits of each of these noncash gifts.

Public and Private Stock Gifts

Public stock is shares of ownership in a public company, such as Coke, Apple, or Netflix. As public stock appreciates over time, you can gift shares of stock tax-free into your donor-advised fund. Once the stock shares are received in your DAF, they are sold, and 100 percent of the proceeds are available for you to give away to your favorite charities. This differs from the less tax-efficient way of selling the stock shares by selling them yourself, paying the capital gains, and then donating what is left to your DAF.

Private stock is ownership of shares in a private company that does not allow the public to purchase stock in the business. These are closely held companies with a small number of shareholders. In a similar fashion to public stock, you can gift private stock into your DAF and liquidate it, with the proceeds available for you to gift to your favorite charities, or you can sell the stock shares, pay the capital gains, and then donate to your DAF, which is less tax efficient.

Real Estate Gifts

A noncash gift of real estate is more complex than donating stocks to your DAF. The property must first be inspected to ensure there is no prior environmental damage to the soil, such as a chemical or oil spill. An analysis of the debt load in the asset is also required to confirm that the property is a viable gift. Like other

51 "About," National Christian Foundation, accessed November 2, 2024, https://www.ncfgiving.com.

noncash gifts, you can either give away to charitable causes the proceeds from the gift into the DAF or give after you sell the real estate. A gift after the sale will be subject to capital gains taxes. Noncash giving like public stock, private stock, and real estate expands your generosity options.

Business Interest Gifts

Business interest gifts are even more complex than private and public stock gifts and real estate gifts. There are more variables to consider during the gift intake process. An understanding of the structure of the business entity, the operational agreement, the company's debt load, its ownership, the valuation of the business, and the timeline of a potential sale of the company are all critical for the viability of the gift. Business owners can donate all or a portion of their business into their donor-advised fund. Once a potential business gift makes its way through NCF's due diligence process and is approved, all parties sign a gift agreement, and the gift is deposited into the owner's DAF. After the company sells, proceeds that reflect the gift amount flow into the donor-advised fund.

Here is an important reminder: A noncash gift must be donated prior to the signing of a binding agreement to sell. Most but not all letters of intent are non-binding. Moreover, two different giving strategies can be used for a business interest gift or a real estate gift: a give-and-sale and a give-and-hold. Let's look at the benefits of each strategy.

Give-and-Sale

A give-and-sale means a potential sale of a business in the near future. In this scenario, a business owner can gift all or a portion of their business ownership into their DAF. Once the company sale closes, the proceeds from the transaction flow into their giving fund based on the amount of the gift. These tax-free dollars can now be given away to approved charities.

Give-and-Hold

The NCF's noncash give-and-hold strategy enables donors to give noncash assets, such as real estate, business interests, or other appreciated assets, to fund charitable causes. Instead of selling these assets directly, donors transfer them to NCF, potentially maximizing tax benefits by avoiding capital gains taxes. NCF may "hold" the asset, managing or renting it until it's optimal to sell, thus maximizing the eventual charitable impact. NCF asset managers sometimes provide back-office support to business operations and, with all business gifts, submit the financial filing requirements with the IRS to be fully compliant.

This strategy gives donors flexibility, tax advantages, and the ability to leverage significant resources for kingdom-focused giving without liquidating valuable assets upfront. The give-and-hold strategy allows families to do their giving while they are living and to leverage the value of their current assets now and not have to wait for the big windfall at the eventual sale of a company.

The give-and-hold strategy allows a fund holder to grow equity ownership in the company within their DAF. Any distributions from the business will flow into the fund based on the percentage of ownership. So, for example, if the fund holds 10 percent equity in the business, a $10,000 distribution from the company would gift $1,000 into the donor-advised fund. Once the business is sold, the proceeds from the sale will also flow into the DAF based on the percentage of ownership. In some cases, 100 percent ownership of the company is donated to the business owner's DAF. The give-and-hold method allows the business to continue as an operating company with the charitable intent of giving away most of the profits from the company.

Prayer: *Lord, grant me wisdom and creativity to use noncash gifts for your glory. Show me how to share my resources in meaningful ways that bless others and advance your kingdom. In Jesus' name. Amen.*

The Power of Generosity: The donor-advised fund and noncash giving facilitate and accelerate generous giving.

Trust in the Lord

Proverbs 3:5, which says, "Trust in the Lord with all your heart, and do not lean on your own understanding" (ESV), is a well-recited truth in the Christian life. Many have used this reassuring verse as a go-to when approaching God, anxious as they stare down an unsure future or grapple with a hard decision. Yet the precise context of this proverb describes a faith-focused life around trusting and honoring the Lord with our resources.

This passage goes on to say, "Honor the Lord with your wealth and with the firstfruits of all your produce; then your barns will be filled with plenty, and your vats will be bursting with wine" (vv. 9–10 ESV). Followers of God were instructed to take the firstfruits of their harvest as an offering to the Lord and to trust him for their barns to be filled with plenty of food and their vats to be bursting with wine. The weather, which is an example of uncontrollable circumstances, and the fruit, which are outcomes, are both in God's hands. In other words, keep the Lord as the focus of your life. Work and honor him; give him the glory for your ability to produce more than you need for the benefit of blessing others.

Verse 7 says, "Be not wise in your own eyes; fear the LORD, and turn away from evil" (ESV). Notice how Solomon's Proverbs 3 transitions from trust in the Lord to fear of the Lord, telling us how to access wisdom. Generous living is a life of trust, honor, and fear of God, leading to wisdom from God so that the fruit of generosity oozes out to sweeten lives like tasty maple syrup over hot pancakes.

The book of James, the "Proverbs of the New Testament," goes a step further to extend the idea of our life as an offering to God since blood-bought believers of Jesus Christ are a kind of firstfruit. "He chose to give us birth through the word of truth, that we might be a kind of firstfruits of all he created" (1:18 NIV). We are no longer our own when we are born into the family of God. Our understanding becomes submissive to the Lord's understanding, and we totally trust the Holy Spirit to direct our paths. Charles Spurgeon beautifully unpacked this idea of first being cleansed by Jesus Christ so we are divinely prepared to be a living sacrifice, a firstfruit for the Lord:

> Our offering of ourselves to God, then, is divinely ordered and should be willingly performed, but it *must be mediatorially presented*. We cannot offer ourselves to God directly—we must come through Jesus Christ. Nothing that you and I can do can be in itself acceptable to the Most High. Christ must wash the stains of our best charities in His precious blood, and He must perfume our most industrious works with His own merit—or else they are not such as the pure and holy God can receive.
>
> I do like to think that I can bring myself by holy self-consecration to the Lord Jesus Christ, and can say to Him, "Here I am, a poor unworthy one, defiled with sin. I want to serve God. I do desire to give Him all my powers, my goods, my hours—but Lord, everything I have is so defiled, and I myself am so polluted, put out that dear hand of Yours that was once outstretched to bleed for sin. Take me into Your hand, and then take me up to Your Father's throne, and say, 'Father, I have brought You a poor sinner's heart. He freely offers to give it, for I have fairly won it, and I present it to you. It is all Yours, it

> is all Mine. Father, help that poor heart, as long as it beats, to live for You. Help it with grace to move hands, and tongue, and feet, and every power that is within it, for Your glory and for Yours alone.'"[52]

What a fabulous prayer of generosity: "Father, help that poor heart, as long as it beats, to live for You. Help it with grace to move hands, and tongue, and feet, and every power that is within it, for Your glory and for Yours alone." My poor heart, broken and spiritually bankrupted, is in need of the riches of God's grace as long as it beats for me to live for him. Also, by grace, move my hands to generously serve, my tongue to give hope to hurting hearts, and my feet to carry the gospel of Jesus Christ to everyone I meet, giving my all in the Lord's strength and for his glory.

Prayer: *Lord, I surrender my life to you completely. Let every part of me be devoted to serving you. May I give all I have for your glory and purpose. In Jesus' name. Amen.*

The Power of Generosity: A life first given to the Lord is a life that gives all for the Lord.

We Never Do Generous Living Alone

My wife and I met Rachel Faulkner Brown soon after we learned of her generous heart for widows. Rachel never set out to advance the kingdom through widows; she just wanted to help the younger versions of women like her.

In 1998, Rachel married her college sweetheart one week after she graduated. Three years after Rachel and Todd married, Todd went to play a game of pickup basketball and had a massive aneurysm in his best friend's driveway. Rachel was left widowed at twenty-three, and Todd met Jesus when he was just twenty-seven.

Being widowed is never on anyone's life plan, but it happens twenty-eight hundred times a day in the US, leaving nearly 11.8 million women alone. Death doesn't discriminate as millions of women, young and old, lose themselves in grief, overwhelmed by the sting of death. Rachel found herself in this very place, crying out to God to save Todd and then crying out again to rescue her from loneliness.

Two years after Todd died, Rachel reconnected with a family friend who had grown up with Todd. Blair Faulkner had camped and vacationed together

52 Charles Haddon Spurgeon, "A Kind of Firstfruits," Spurgeon Gems, sermon given January 5, 1868, PDF, 6–7, https://www.spurgeongems.org.

with Todd, and he had hundreds of pictures to prove the connection clearly orchestrated by God. As a child growing up in a small southern Alabama town, Blair had one dream—to fly jets. While he was at the pinnacle of his career flying in the A-10 Thunderbolt II, a.k.a. the "Warthog," out of Naval Air Station Joint Reserve Base New Orleans, Rachel and Blair married in a full military wedding. Not a single attendee escaped the tears of joy laced with grief for what was lost and for the redemption found in their midst.

Blair and Rachel started their family by welcoming their son, Davis, in 2005 and daughter, Campbell, in 2007. Blair was flying the T-38 at Columbus Air Force Base, training the next generation of fighter pilots. On a beautiful spring day, Rachel received the call that she never thought would happen again.

"Rachel, we are looking for you," the base chaplain explained.

Rachel raced to the naval base with two babies in her back seat to hear from the wing commander that Blair and his student pilot had taken off and immediately crashed. Rachel was widowed again, this time with two children under two. It's hard to imagine being widowed once at a young age, but twice might seem like a cruel punishment to an outsider. But Rachel knew immediately something bigger was happening. She presented the gospel at Blair's memorial, and thousands heard the truth at his funeral. God was working it out for good even though she wouldn't see it for years.

Rachel knew she had a unique opportunity financially and spiritually again. She had a learned understanding of giving, having been raised in a generous tithing family and having faced loss once and needing to steward a small inheritance. Rachel had seen her family live their life as if nothing they owned was theirs. She saw her grandparents' wisdom in business and her parents' generosity to her friends and her own ambitions, and she caught a lot more than she was actually taught. No debt except the house was always the theme.

Widows with windfalls of money can go one of two ways: They can hoard in fear or give in grace. Rachel chose grace, and as she moved toward generosity in complete faith, she couldn't outgive God, and the Lord was meeting her in the secret places in the valley of her pain. She understood, like her parents, that what she had inherited in death was not hers. It was all the Lord's. She remarried five years after losing Blair to a consultant and pastor in Atlanta who also shared the same views on generosity. Rod was giving over 20 percent of his income when they met, and Rachel knew immediately, before she ever saw a balance sheet, that what Rod had was not his.

In 2014, Rachel began a ministry with fifty chairs from IKEA and a Bluetooth speaker—no board of directors, no 501(c)(3), just faith. She wanted women to have a place to share their stories and worship. She wanted prayer to be the center of the night, and she wanted to have a place where any woman from any church could hear a story that empowered her heart to believe that if God did it for Rachel, he could do it for her.

Little did she know that this small beginning was part of a much bigger plan to impact the world for widows like herself. After years of just managing the ministry on her own, Rachel reluctantly applied for her 501(c)(3) tax-exempt status. Rod had encouraged Rachel that keeping the organization to what she could manage on her own was selfish and not God's best plan if she really wanted to impact the kingdom. In 2018, she had the idea to start an outreach arm of the ministry called Never Alone Widows, a retreat for the widows across this country who are raising children on their own. That retreat turned into a haven for thousands of widows who meet every month through local groups in over one hundred cities. Through retreats and national conferences, women who have convinced themself they are alone in their mourning discover that they are not.

Rachel has seen hundreds of widows get baptized into a new life with Jesus, free from shame and crippling grief. She has taken the model to Poland for refugee widows, and women who have experienced Never Alone Widows have gone to Uganda to love on hundreds of widows with the gospel.

When Rachel started the official ministry in 2017, she heard the Lord tell her to give away the first $10,000 she received. She knew that obedience to his voice was the only path she could take. She still believes to this day that it was a test of trust that met her deep-rooted faith. Rachel's goal is for widows across the United States to be the most generous group of women in the world. She wants every widow to understand generosity in her bones because Rachel believes God's generosity to her unleashed a healing of a nation through widows. Rachel's generous living helps widows never to be alone.

Prayer: *Lord, may my generosity bring comfort and strength to those on difficult paths. Help me share my blessings and experience and ease their burdens as they journey forward. In Jesus' name. Amen.*

The Power of Generosity: Generosity helps others who are traveling down a similarly rough road.

Receiving Allows Another to Be Blessed

When you receive, you can be generous by giving another the gift of being blessed. Giving and receiving are the rhythm of a faithful follower of Jesus Christ. The promise of blessing is attached to both. Giving results in the bigger blessing, but receiving involves being blessed as well. Next to the gift of salvation in Jesus Christ, love is the greatest gift to give or receive. Both giving love and receiving love are necessary to experience the fullness of Christ's love and his followers. Some, especially the self-reliant, struggle with receiving because they fear being a burden or maybe they feel embarrassed, but in God's heart for generous living, being a receiver means you are being blessed by the Lord. You are allowing another to experience a bigger blessing.

I introduced you to Scott Bowen in chapter 5. When he was young, Scott was one of four men who showed up to our home, having been commissioned by their church's small group leader to serve our family. The bulging truck and trailer that showed up at our modest, needy house were adorned and overflowing with a variety of plants, shrubs, flowers, and pine-straw bales. The mission of these generous young men was to do a landscaping makeover that reminds me of today's home and yard remodel TV shows, in which teams convert a tired house into a warm, inviting home. Our new curb appeal made my wife and four daughters squeal with delightful gratitude. A predictable outcome of generous deeds! To our amazement and grateful hearts, all the foliage, flowers, and labor were timely, beautiful gifts.

Our modest budget did not include this robust level of lovely landscaping that felt like an extravagance to us. And I have to confess, my pride struggled to receive this generous, extravagant gift. But God reminded me that this was his generous provision through his generous people. Our family recalled the words of Paul that whatever level of blessing and joy we were feeling, our benefactors were experiencing many times more since the giver is more blessed than the receiver (Acts 20:35). Instead of being prideful and denying my bride and our generous friends a blessing, I celebrated the Lord's gift to our family with the multicolor parade of his breathtaking floral creation. His glory radiated in brilliant delight for him and for all who would experience God's gift to us.

I kept up with Scott over the years since his generous deed that day because my daughter Rachel was good friends with Cara, Scott's sister. His dad, Howard, became a role model to me and many others with his generous, private acts of kindness and his gift to build our new church building without a markup or fee.

Our church was born and launched because of generous hearts like Howard's. And generosity, like a common cold, infected the family. Scott's mom, Doris, was also a selfless leader in the community, teaching women's Bible studies.

Scott and his friends were a great lesson to me and my family of being willing to graciously receive as a blessing to those who want to generously give.

In Acts, Paul gave his farewell address to the leaders of the early church: "I commit you to God and to the word of his grace, which can build you up and give you an inheritance....I have not coveted anyone's silver or gold or clothing....We must help the weak, remembering the words the Lord Jesus himself said: 'It is more blessed to give than to receive'" (20:32–33, 35 NIV). He committed them to God and to the word of his grace so they could live for God. He went on to explain how he had modeled a life of generosity, not being greedy, and then quoted Jesus on the blessing of giving and receiving. In the Gospels, Jesus also warned against various types of greed (Luke 12:15).

Money competes with our devotion to God and must be given away to free us from its unhealthy control. Tim Keller made a helpful point when he said, "People say, 'Oh, money's an idol.' Well, yeah, okay. But I think it'd be a little more accurate to say your money reveals your idols."[53] Like Paul, we finish well when we have lived a life of generosity as a preventative to greedy, idolatrous living.

Where are you on the continuum of giving and receiving? Giving may be a very natural expression of your gratitude to God, or you may be overly cautious about not giving away too much for fear of not having enough. On the other end of the spectrum, receiving may come easy to you because you understand the joy others receive by allowing them to bless you, and you are comfortable with the community of other Christ followers loving you well. Consider how the Lord may want to grow you as a giver and a receiver. Blessings are reserved for both.

Begin by becoming a generous receiver of love from God and others. Henri Nouwen spoke to this point: "The question of receiving the love of Christ is really very important. I personally feel more and more that sometimes it is harder for us to fully receive love than to give it. I am more and more convinced that we will find the peace and joy of Christ when we let him truly enter into the deepest places of our heart, especially those places where we are afraid, insecure, and self-rejecting."[54]

---

53 Tim Keller, "The Gospel, Grace, and Giving," Generous Giving, posted November 15, 2015, Vimeo video, 16:00, https://vimeo.com.

54 Henri Nouwen, "Let Him Love You," Henri Nouwen Society, September 5, 2023, https://henrinouwen.org.

If receiving and giving are difficult for you, remember this promise: "Give, and you will receive. Your gift will return to you in full—pressed down, shaken together to make room for more, running over, and poured into your lap. The amount you give will determine the amount you get back" (Luke 6:38 NLT).

Prayer: *Heavenly Father, I am so grateful for your good gifts in my life. Lead me to give as you give. In Jesus' name. Amen.*

The Power of Generosity: Giving and receiving love are the foundation of a life blessed to bless others.

Sell All You Have...Really?

Jesus said to the rich young man, "One thing you still lack. Sell all that you have and distribute to the poor, and you will have treasure in heaven; and come, follow me" (Luke 18:22 ESV).

When my friend Bill began his business career, his objective was to be rich and retire early. However, in his late fifties, he and his wife found themselves living in a garage apartment. They had freed themselves from the stuff that kept them from experiencing the fullness of what the Lord had for them.

Since he grew up in a strong Christian home, Bill had heard all the Bible stories, including the one where Jesus told the rich man to sell all his possessions, give to the poor, and follow him. As a young man, Bill made the decision to follow Jesus, which was the best decision Bill ever made, but the thought of selling everything and giving to the poor seemed a bit unrealistic. Why did it matter anyway? Bill never thought he'd be considered a "rich man."

Over the course of Bill's multidecade business career, however, God blessed Bill. When he retired at age fifty-four, Bill's objective was to perfect his golf game, which, after six months, resulted in him feeling frustrated with life—and his golf game had gotten worse! After breaking a golf club over his knee during a particularly bad round of golf and upon the advice of his wife, Bill sought counsel from his pastor who, in so many words, told Bill he was stuck in neutral and that wasn't the way God created him. Who could have imagined that two months later, Bill would be serving in a leadership role at Generous Giving? This organization encourages those entrusted with much to lay up treasure in heaven and take hold of the life that is truly life. This began a season of Bill's life that, in many ways, was more fruitful and rewarding than his business career.

During his career, Bill had been somewhat generous while at the same time accumulating a lot of stuff. His idea of living comfortably led to a life of complexity, which included always maintaining and fixing the stuff. While serving at Generous Giving, Bill heard God ask him to focus on what he should keep rather than what he should give. During a planning retreat that Bill and his wife took, God asked Bill and his wife the "rich young ruler question": *Will you sell all your possessions, give to the poor, and follow me more deeply?* The impression from God was so significant that Bill and his wife sold their two houses and most of the furniture and gave away a substantial amount of the proceeds. All the stuff they had left were two cars and furniture that fit in his son's garage, and for several months, Bill and his wife lived in the garage apartment of some close friends. On one occasion during that time, Bill's wife said, "I knew we married for better or for worse, but I didn't think we'd be homeless in our fifties!"

After several months of seeking God's direction, Bill and his wife bought a home much more suited to their desired future lifestyle. Shortly after, through God's providence, Bill transitioned to a leadership role at the National Christian Foundation, where he served for five years until his wife passed away. God then led him to serve his family and to a deeper abiding in Jesus.

Of course, as we seek Jesus first, Jesus always leads us in paths of righteousness, and soon God divinely led Bill to meet and marry an amazing, godly woman whose husband had passed away. Bill now serves on staff at his church, encouraging others to lay up treasures in heaven and take hold of life that is truly life. Now in his seventies, Bill understands the significance of seeking God first, and the result is a life of incredible adventure.

The Power of Generosity: One life of generosity can become impactful when freed from complicated living to a life available to love others well.

Delight in Decluttered Living

Paul understood the clutter of a culture that demanded attention from a religious leader of his status. He criticized the cluttered lifestyle with an intellectual air that left many amused and amazed. "I also count all things loss for the excellence of the knowledge of Christ Jesus my Lord, for whom I have suffered the loss of all things, and count them as rubbish, that I may gain Christ" (Philippians 3:8 NKJV). Once a driven crusader against Christ, Paul encountered Jesus Christ personally and became a crusader for him. Because of his radical change of heart, Paul sacrificed his résumé of accomplishments on the dung heap of earthly desires in exchange for knowing Christ "and the power of His resurrection, and the fellowship of His sufferings" (v. 10 NKJV). Paul found great delight in decluttering his life for his Lord. He expunged the nonessential—becoming famous—and embraced the essential—making Jesus famous.

I catch myself enjoying the ease of swiping my phone screen and, just like that, ordering stuff: books, gadgets, and more books. But do I really need more stuff to clutter up and complicate my life? Am I as conscious of setting my affections above with the recentering of my soul as I am at swiping my phone? My cluttered life can lose its edge of effectiveness for Christ. I have to reset my mind and affections above, so I send ahead treasures that outlast trivial trinkets I will leave behind.

Has your life become cluttered with trivial matters and less meaningful stuff? What is your plan to regularly declutter your calendar, closets, and checkbook to reflect the heart of Christ? Pray about a practical process to place boundaries around your tendency to spend too much on earthly possessions. Replace this temptation with a routine to direct your resources toward the true riches of treasure in heaven. A regular trip to a thrift store that supports Christian ministry is a good habit to cultivate. You can drop off your overaccumulation of stuff and, at the same time, support kingdom initiatives. Consider decluttering to become a more focused disciple of Christ.

Most of all, you will find the greatest delight by elevating your affections upward toward the lover of your soul, Jesus Christ. A life surrendered to Jesus does not allow other competitors to gain unhealthy influence over the physical, spiritual, and emotional aspects of life. The increased filling of your calendar can subtly suck the life from your soul if you are not intentional to keep time for Spirit-led refreshment. Immerse yourself in God's creation to refresh faith in your heart and allow the experience of the divine to grow you in grace and understanding toward a focused life of generosity. Your affections immersed in the love of Christ provide clarity by decluttering a conflicted mind, freeing you for generous living.

> That means you can sell your possessions and give generously to the poor. You can have a different kind of savings plan: one that never depreciates, one that never defaults, one that can't be plundered by crooks or destroyed by natural calamities. Your treasure will be stored in the heavens, and since your treasure is there, your heart will be lodged there as well.

> I'm not just talking theory. There is urgency in all this. If you're apathetic and complacent, then you'll miss the moment of opportunity. (Luke 12:33–36 VOICE)

Prayer: *Heavenly Father, remind me to reassess and release my stuff so I am free from the bondage of materialism. In Jesus' name. Amen.*

The Power of Generosity: Giving away material possessions can free you to better serve the Lord and others.

The Shepherd's Fund

Those who live generously will also sometimes need the support of others who are following their example of generous living. God's servants who shepherd the church are generous by their very nature. Shepherds over God's flock have very real needs that we sometimes miss. Gratefully, the Lord laid on the heart of a generous giver to prosper these leaders by providing for their practical needs.

The Shepherd's Fund aptly describes this creative, generous initiative to care for pastors. A few years back, a family foundation inquired of the National Christian Foundation to assist in a strategy to serve retired pastors who struggle to pay their medical bills. We met with the head of the foundation, brainstormed, and planned for over a year before coming up with a process to pilot a donor-advised fund at NCF. We also partnered with Helping Hands, a ministry that specializes in hardship cases.

Collaboratively, we designed a due diligence process to review Shepherd's Fund applications from retired pastors. Pastors who qualify for assistance can receive up to $10,000 to cover their medical bills. Over time, the Shepherd's Fund moved to work exclusively with Helping Hands, with NCF still involved as an advocate and encourager.[55] As the generosity footprint of the Shepherd's Fund expanded, NCF was able to introduce to the Shepherd's Fund a longtime friend and colleague in ministry, Charles Buffington.

Charles Buffington became fast friends with Robert Beckum, a former pastor who oversaw the Shepherd's Fund. With his years of influence within churches, Charles introduced the Shepherd's Fund to a large network of Black churches and pastors. The vision grew from helping retired pastors to helping up-and-coming pastors enrolled in seminary. So today there are $10,000 scholarships for Black pastors in training that can be applied toward their seminary

55 For more information, visit https://www.theshepherdsfund.org.

education to help them avoid a significant debt load from student loans.[56] The Shepherd's Fund is a compelling example of a generous vision to help pastors who are normally the ones helping others. Their generosity is refreshing these servants of the Lord with tender care.

Oh, the joy of generous living! My prayer is that after reading this chapter, you will open your heart and imagination to how the Lord wants to direct your daily life to be a blessing to others—yes, to be a blessing waiting to happen! As you have been inspired, ask the Holy Spirit what he has for you and how you can join him in being available for intentional, generous living.

Prayer: *Lord, help me supply resources to and support those who sacrifice for others. May my generosity refresh their spirits and bring renewed strength to their selfless work. In Jesus' name. Amen.*

The Power of Generosity: Giving resources to those who sacrifice their lives to give to others refreshes the generous.

Spontaneous Giving

I was recently touched by a story of generosity that appears in *The Grapes of Wrath* by John Steinbeck. As one of Steinbeck's most famous books, it won the Pulitzer Prize for fiction and was cited prominently when he was awarded the Nobel Prize in Literature in 1962. The book takes place during the Great Depression, which resulted in many people migrating to different areas of the US. One such migrant family was making their way from Oklahoma to California in search of work. A riveting scene on the family's road trip showcases spontaneous generosity.

In a diner, a waitress, Mae, is serving two truck drivers when a famished family from Oklahoma enters. They're clearly poor, wearing only patched overalls. After Mae finally relents to giving the father some bread for ten cents, the father pulls out a penny along with the dime. The father looks down at his two sons, who are eyeing the candy case, and asks Mae if the striped candy is penny candy.

She replies, "Oh—them. Well, no—them's two for a penny."[57]

Only after the father and his sons leave does one of the truck drivers say, "Them was a nickel apiece candy."[58]

56 "The Need," The Shepherd's Fund, accessed November 3, 2024, https://www.theshepherdsfund.org.

57 John Steinbeck, *The Grapes of Wrath* (Penguin Publishing Group, 2006), 161.

58 Steinbeck, *Grapes of Wrath*, 161.

Soon after, the two truck drivers leave the diner, each dropping a coin on the counter. Even though their meal only cost fifteen cents apiece, both paid with half dollars.

As I imagined these characters in the diner and read their conversation, my jaw dropped, my heart was strangely warmed, and my mind was animated by the responses of spontaneous generosity that spurred each other to give. Most of us will or have experienced each person's circumstance in this story. We can empathize with the needy family suffering from financial challenges and the fear of significant change. Perhaps you see yourself in the people working hard to try to keep their business afloat, yet when face-to-face with the very real needs of another human being, they show compassion and generosity. And as they are refreshing the less fortunate, the more fortunate truck drivers are blessing them right back.

Who are you in this story? And where is the Lord taking you in his great adventure of generous living? Keep loving generously and trusting God to provide beyond what you could ever ask or think. Generous living is faith living, and both are where you journey with Jesus on the great adventure of the abundant living he promises.

Summary of "Living Generously"

- Fear and doubt take flight when, as God's beloved children, we stay faithful in our generosity and trust him for his very best.
- The donor-advised fund and noncash giving facilitate and accelerate generous giving.
- A life first given to the Lord is a life that gives all for the Lord.
- Generosity helps others who are traveling down a similarly rough road.
- Giving and receiving love are the foundation of a life blessed to bless others.
- One life of generosity can become impactful when freed from complicated living to a life available to love others well.
- Giving away material possessions can free you to better serve the Lord and others.
- Giving resources to those who sacrifice their lives to give to others refreshes the generous.

A Generous Prayer

Dear God, grant me a generous spirit that mirrors your abundant grace. Help me see every possession as a gift from you, entrusted to me for the benefit of others. Guide my heart to give freely, not out of obligation but out of love and gratitude for your blessings. May my generosity extend beyond material wealth, encompassing my time, talents, and compassion. Let my life reflect your boundless generosity and inspire others to embrace the joy of selfless giving. In your name, I pray for the courage to live generously and make a meaningful difference in the world. Amen.

Epilogue

The Generous Work of the Holy Spirit

Generosity is a journey, a journey of experiencing the rich salvation of Jesus Christ, the abundant wisdom of your heavenly Father, and the gracious comfort of the Holy Spirit. Whether you are young or old in the faith, you have the opportunity to grow in the grace of giving through the power of the Spirit. Before Jesus ascended to heaven, he promised he would send the Comforter (John 16:7). He went on to explain how the Holy Spirit would guide us in truth (v. 13), glorify Jesus, and give to us what is the Father's and the Son's (v. 15). That is generous indeed! The Holy Spirit fills and empowers you for God's glory. But to access the Holy Spirit's power requires you to surrender and receive his fullness into your life.

Dependence on the Spirit's power is like the need for electric vehicles to have an ongoing charge. Electric vehicles are quiet, dependable, and powerful as long as they have received a proper charge. After 250 to 350 miles, a driver must stop and recharge to continue driving. The same is true for the power of generosity at work in your life. Moment-by-moment surrender to the Spirit is the spiritual charge that you need to experience the riches of God's generosity, which empowers and motivates you to radical generosity. Generosity becomes as natural as breathing as you inhale the Spirit's power and exhale competing desires. Humility helps you stay plugged into the power of the Holy Spirit.

Honestly ask yourself this: Are you satisfied with "the forgiveness of sins, according to the riches of His grace" (Ephesians 1:7 NKJV), when the Lord would also give you "according to the riches of His glory, to be strengthened with might through His Spirit in the inner man" (3:16)? The power of genuine generosity begins with the grace-filled work of the Holy Spirit at the inception of your salvation, is extended by the generous work of the Spirit in your surrendered life, and comes to fruition with the gentle work of the Spirit in your inner being that reveals the riches of God's glory.

You may not feel like your motives for giving are 100 percent pure, but that's okay. Stay on the generosity path, and the Lord will purify your intentions. Your motives for giving are made right when you are right with God and right with others. Submit to Jesus as your sin bearer, the Holy Spirit as your burden bearer, and your heavenly Father as your fruit bearer. Ah, the Trinity's sweet, generous love!

Others may question your generous ways, but you answer only to the one who is the way and who shows you the way. Love is your guide as your life of love joyfully travels on the road of generosity, looking to refresh and be refreshed.

Prayer: *I come before you, generous Father, humbled by your boundless grace. Fill me with your Holy Spirit, which ignites hearts to embrace generosity. May your love flow through me, allowing me to touch lives with compassion and kindness. Grant me eyes to see opportunities to give freely just as you have given to me abundantly. Strengthen my faith so that I may trust in your provision as I extend my hands in service. May my acts of generosity reflect your love and shine brightly in a world longing for hope. Through your Spirit working within me, may I be a vessel of your blessings, spreading joy and transforming lives all for your glory. In Jesus' name. Amen.*

Generosity Resources

A Theology of Generosity: 2 Corinthians 8–9

- Generosity is unrelated to income and wealth: "In the midst of a very severe trial, their overflowing joy and their extreme poverty welled up in rich generosity" (8:2 NIV).
- Generosity is never forced: "I testify that they gave as much as they were able, and even beyond their ability. Entirely on their own" (8:3 NIV).
- Generosity cannot be contained: "They urgently pleaded with us for the privilege of sharing in this service to the Lord's people" (8:4 NIV).
- Generosity is always focused first toward the Lord: "They gave themselves first of all to the Lord, and then by the will of God also to us" (8:5 NIV).
- Generosity is tangible evidence of our love for God: "I am not commanding you, but I want to test the sincerity of your love" (8:8 NIV).
- Generous people meet needs: "At the present time your plenty will supply what they need, so that in turn their plenty will supply what you need.... 'The one who gathered much did not have too much, and the one who gathered little did not have too little'" (8:14–15 NIV).
- Generosity honors the Lord: "What is more, he was chosen by the churches to accompany us as we carry the offering, which we administer in order to honor the Lord himself and to show our eagerness to help" (8:19 NIV).

- Real generosity is expressed cheerfully: "Each of you should give what you have decided in your heart to give, not reluctantly or under compulsion, for God loves a cheerful giver" (9:7 NIV).
- Generosity is personal between us and God: "Each of you should give what you have decided in your heart to give, not reluctantly or under compulsion, for God loves a cheerful giver" (9:7 NIV).
- God provides the gift for the generous to give: "He who supplies seed to the sower and bread for food will also supply and increase your store of seed and will enlarge the harvest of your righteousness. You will be enriched in every way so that you can be generous" (9:10–11 NIV).
- Expressed generosity moves others closer to God: "So that you can be generous…and through us your generosity will result in thanksgiving to God. This service that you perform is not only supplying the needs of the Lord's people but is also overflowing in many expressions of thanks to God. Because of the service by which you have proved yourselves, others will praise God for the obedience that accompanies your confession of the gospel of Christ, and for your generosity" (9:11–13 NIV).[59]

Organizations Providing Resources for Generous Living

- Generous Giving: generousgiving.com
    - ▹ A Generosity Conversation
    - ▹ A Journey of Generosity
    - ▹ A Celebration of Generosity
    - ▹ Generosity video stories (three to ten minutes each)
- The National Christian Foundation: ncfgiving.com
    - ▹ A Giving Fund
    - ▹ A Giving Strategy
- Wisdom Hunters: wisdomhunters.com

59 This resource was developed by the Christian Stewardship Network. Used with permission. For more information, visit https://www.christianstewardshipnetwork.com.

A Family Giving Strategy

Trudy Cathy White (daughter of Jeannette and S. Truett Cathy, founder of Chick-fil-A), in her very helpful book *A Legacy That Lasts*,[60] outlines wise and practical guidelines for giving. Here is her overview:

Spouses Must Work Together on Giving Decisions

"Discussions about when, where, how, and how much to give are some of the richest, most rewarding talks John and I ever have. These opportunities can make you and your spouse truly feel like a team that God has put together. Yes, this can lead to some disagreements, but the bottom line is that we do not make giving decisions without the consent of the other. This one guideline has probably been the most important principle we've followed regarding our giving."[61]

Narrow Your Giving

"Knowing what matters to us provides guardrails to help focus our giving, and that's especially important when it comes to saying no to a good cause. Again, you can't support every charity, so identify what you specifically care about and point your giving dollars in that direction."[62]

Be Specific and Intentional

"It's a special blessing to be on the receiving end of a thoughtful gift. Just last week as I write this, I spoke at a training event with those who serve in different areas of volunteer leadership for summer camp. They presented me with a small gift as a token of appreciation. It was my very own Nesquick (formerly Nestlé Quik) tumbler for mixing chocolate milk. Now, you should understand that I absolutely love chocolate milk. It's one of my favorite things in the world. What

60 Trudy Cathy White, *A Legacy That Lasts: Preserving and Transferring Your Family Values* (Forefronts Books, 2023).

61 White, *A Legacy That Lasts*, 128.

62 White, *A Legacy That Lasts*, 129–30.

made this little gift so special is not just they gave me something I knew I would enjoy; they gave me something they knew I would enjoy. They had taken the time to know my personal likes and dislikes, and they went to the trouble of picking out a little something for me. That kind of personalization means the world."[63]

Plan Your Giving for the Year

"Generosity isn't only about stewarding money; you're also trying to give your time, talent, and opportunities of influence. These can be difficult decisions if you're trying to make them on the fly. Life gets pretty crazy for most of us, so it's best not to leave your giving decisions to chance or to your whims in the heat of the moment. For that reason, John and I sit down with our calendar once a year and block out time specifically for acts of generosity throughout the year."[64]

Fund Your Children's Giving When Necessary

"Teaching young children how to give can be tricky, especially since they don't often have much money of their own. Whenever possible, then, we recommend funding their giving by giving them money and teaching them how to use it generously for others."[65]

Teach Children How to Be Generous with Their Words

"One aspect of giving that often goes unnoticed is how to be generous with our words. Being generous in our speech—such as with encouragement, thanks, compliments, and words of support and affirmation—is something anyone can do, regardless of who they are, how old they are, where they live, or how much they have.... [We teach our grandchildren] that our words have to be positive and encouraging. That means we do not allow the children to whine, complain, or tattle on their siblings or cousins.... Teaching children how to be gracious and generous with their words is one of the greatest gifts you can give their future spouse!"[66]

---

63 White, *A Legacy That Lasts*, 131.
64 White, *A Legacy That Lasts*, 132.
65 White, *A Legacy That Lasts*, 133.
66 White, *A Legacy That Lasts*, 134–35.

Progressively Involve Your Children as They Get Older

"Involve your children in opportunities that are appropriate for their age. When they're very young, for instance, you should let them engage in specific, narrow ways they can more easily understand. For example, when we first moved to Brazil, none of us could speak the language very well. That made it difficult for us to truly become part of the community and get to know their needs. However, two very obvious needs in the community near us were poverty and hunger. So, one of the first things we did to get to know our neighbors was cook a huge pot of rice and beef stew. Our plan was to go throughout the community and offer our new neighbors a free meal for their family."[67]

Do Due Diligence

"While I strongly encourage you to give generously, I do not want you to give blindly. Dig in, get to know the organization and/or the specific project you're giving to, look at how they spend their money, find out how much of their donations go to people in need versus 'administrative cost,' and give wisely. The money you give away will be some of the most important investments you ever make, because you're investing in the kingdom of God and in the lives of His children. Don't throw your money away on organizations that will either waste or pocket your donations."[68]

Do Your Giving While You're Living

"So much of our giving is traditionally tied up in our dying (i.e., our estate plans). It is a wonderful thing to leave your wealth to the people and causes you cherish, but don't save it all for after your death. Give while you're still living to see the blessings of your giving in action."[69]

Public or Private Giving

"I've never been comfortable doing a lot of giving 'out in the open.' John and I have mostly followed the Matthew 6:3 principle: 'When you give to someone in need, don't let your left hand know what your right hand is doing' (NLT). That is, don't make a big show of your act of giving. I'd say we have done this for the

67 White, *A Legacy That Lasts*, 135.
68 White, *A Legacy That Lasts*, 138.
69 White, *A Legacy That Lasts*, 138–39.

vast majority of our giving—especially our financial giving—for two good reasons: It's what the Bible tells us to do (Matthew 6:3). So that God (not us) gets all the glory. This policy has worked well for us in general, but we've most recently been challenged to use our giving as a way to inspire others to give. And that has indeed been a bit of a challenge for us.

"When you give openly, you have the opportunity to make it known that you believe the money is the Lord's and that He has given it to you to manage. You can keep the focus on Him and make it clear that you view yourself only as the channel through which He is giving this gift. Making that known can be a huge incentive for others, and it's a win-win-win for you, the other giver, and the cause you're both supporting—as long as you keep your heart humble and focused on the Lord. That said, there's still nothing quite like the fun of anonymously leaving a $100 tip on a $10 restaurant bill and running out the door before the server knows what's happening!"[70]

---

70 White, *A Legacy That Lasts*, 139–40.

Interviews on Generosity with Howard Dayton, Ron Blue, and Terry Parker

Howard Dayton

Howard is the founder of Crown Ministries and Compass, both organizations with a mission to engage followers of Christ in Bible studies on financial stewardship and generosity. In 2014, Asbury University dedicated their business school to Howard and his wife, Beverly, a couple best characterized by "service and sacrifice," according to their friends.[71]

In June 2024, Howard was kind enough to engage in an informal Q and A with me. The following are his answers to my questions, which he has given me permission to include in this book.[72]

1. Do you think being part of a like-minded community plays a part in your generosity story? And what does that look like in your life?

Howard: Huge part! I've been blessed to lead more than eighty Crown, and now Compass, small group studies. In each group, we spend a week studying giving, and because the leader learns more than anyone else, I've learned a lot about being generous. Also, I have some very close friends. We've been meeting together for more than thirty years, and they are extraordinarily generous. Their example has rubbed off.

2. Which verses inspire your generosity? Why?

Howard: There are several. John 3:16 says, "God so loved the world that he gave his one and only Son" Jesus to die for us (NIV). God is a giver, and we should be too. Luke 12:34 says, "Where your treasure is, there your heart will be also" (NIV). So give each gift to the glory of Christ. The foundation to all my giving is

71 "Howard Dayton School of Business," Asbury University, accessed July 29, 2024, https://www.asbury.edu.

72 Interview has been edited for clarity.

found in 1 Chronicles 29:11–12: "Everything in the heavens and earth is your, O Lord, and this is your kingdom. We adore you as being in control of everything. Riches and honor come from you alone, and you are the ruler of all mankind; your hand controls power and might, and it is at your discretion that men are made great and given strength" (TLB).

God is the owner; we're just stewards of what he's given us. So it's our responsibility to be faithful in handling money his way.

3. How would you encourage others who are on their own journey of generosity?

Howard: There is no substitute for learning what the Bible says about giving. This is what changed me from a person who never gave to one who loves generosity. So ask the Lord to bring some friends into your life who are generous, and if you want to participate a Compass small group study, visit compassfinancialministry.org.

4. Being generous comes with a cost. Can you share a story where generosity cost you something dear?

Howard: I'm eighty now, and when I was thirty years old, it felt as if my generosity was costing me big-time! But now, it never feels as if it is costing me anything. It's not mine, and I'm going to be face-to-face with Christ soon. Also, I've had a lifetime of experiencing God's provision even when giving sacrificially. He is always faithful.

5. If you had an epitaph about generosity, what would you want it to read?

Howard: *God loved, and he gave. Howard loved, and he gave.*

Ron Blue

Ron Blue is the founder and cofounder of several organizations, including the Ron Blue Institute; the Ronald Blue and Company, which is now Ronald Blue Trust; Kingdom Advisors, a ministry that educates Christian financial professionals on biblical wisdom; and the National Christian Foundation, a ministry that helps people develop biblical generosity strategies.

Ron Blue was also generous in responding to my email Q and A in June 2024 and has given me permission to share his answers here.[73]

73 Interview has been edited for clarity.

1. Do you think being part of a like-minded community plays a part in your generosity story? And what does that look like in your life?

Ron: Without question, being associated with some type of community that shares the same giving convictions is an encouragement in my own life. My personal mission statement, which the Lord impressed upon me in 1979, is "to help Christians plan and manage their finances so that they would have more financial resources available to help fund the fulfillment of the Great Commission." As such, I have been working with hundreds and hundreds of Christians over the years in developing giving plans. Their stories and convictions have always been an encouragement to me as I am confronted daily with men and women who desire to give at a maximum level.

2. Which verses inspire your generosity? Why?

Ron: When I have the privilege of signing books, I always use the same verse, 2 Corinthians 8:9: "You know the grace of our Lord Jesus Christ, that though he was rich, yet for your sake he became poor, so that you by his poverty might become rich" (ESV). In the Sermon on the Mount, Jesus said, "Give to him who asks you, and from him who wants to borrow from you do not turn away" (Matthew 5:42 NKJV). The other passage that I find very convicting regarding giving is 1 Chronicles 29. The whole chapter describes the authentic giver beautifully. This is a passage that is worth reading frequently.

3. How would you encourage others who are on their own journey of generosity?

Ron: Having worked with so many givers over the years, I would state that unequivocally, giving is the only way to break the power of money. Secondly, giving must be the priority use of money. And lastly, unless you set some finish lines on lifestyle and financial independence, you will never give maximally.

4. Being generous comes with a cost. Can you share a story where generosity cost you something dear?

Ron: Giving always costs you something in that you are giving something of worth that you own or possess that you could use in many ways. I remember so vividly that at one point, Judy and I decided to give our vacation savings to a ministry rather than use it for a long-planned vacation. God, by his grace, replaced that vacation with multiple free vacations over the years. For many years, we never paid for a vacation because a friend who owned a lake home allowed our family to use it every summer.

5. If you had an epitaph about generosity, what would you want it to read?

Ron: As I have committed my life to helping others give, God called me to start or help start several organizations focused on giving. I have now lived long enough to see the fruit of those organizations, and it is beyond my comprehension what God has done. So I would say an epitaph for me personally would be *He planted, many others watered, and God gave the increase.*

Terry Parker

Terry founded the National Christian Foundation in 1982 with Ron Blue and Larry Burkett. Terry retired from his law firm in 2003 to devote himself full-time to NCF. Terry and his wife, Paula, reside in Atlanta and have three children and nine grandchildren.

Below are Terry's responses to my email questions, which he generously supplied in July 2024 and which he has granted me permission to quote here.[74]

1. Do you think being part of a like-minded community plays a part in your generosity story? And what does that look like in your life?

Terry: Being connected to a fellowship of Christians in my teenage years, right as I was wrestling with my salvation, enabled me to learn the starting point of good stewardship, and that is the tithe. From the first time I ever earned a dollar, 10 percent went to the church. And that has been true for me for seventy years. I would not have learned that lesson without a crowd of witnesses surrounding me.

2. Which verses inspire your generosity? Why?

Terry: Two of the verses that have inspired my and my wife's stewardship are Proverbs 19:17—"Whoever is generous to the poor lends to the Lord, and he will repay" (ESV)—and 1 Timothy 6:18—"They should give much to those in need and be ready to share" (NLV). We have made it a lifelong practice to find people with whom to share what God has entrusted to us. We have bought cars for single moms, full-time Christian workers, and missionaries. We have given exorbitant gratuities in the name of Jesus. We have paid for families to take

74 Interview has been edited for clarity.

vacations when they couldn't afford to do so on their own. And we have had the privilege of doing many other acts of kindness as God gives us opportunity.

3. How would you encourage others who are on their own journey of generosity?

Terry: I have always encouraged others to find opportunities to share without expecting anything in return as God gives them the opportunity to.

4. Being generous comes with a cost. Can you share a story where generosity cost you something dear?

Terry: When Paula and I first got married, for the only time in our married life, we dropped our giving to the basic 10 percent level. A client of mine stole $15,000 from me, resulting in my needing to borrow a large sum of money from the bank. For three years, the payment to the bank took all but $67 a month from our margin. This became all we had for eating out, taking a vacation, going to the movies, or doing anything that cost money. It never even occurred to us to stop tithing, and we learned a lot about the wonderful places we could go that don't cost money, such as state and federal parks.

5. If you had an epitaph about generosity, what would you want it to read?

Terry: *God provided not only for his every need but also an abundance for him to give away.*

Discussion Guide

Format

This discussion guide for *The Power of Generosity* is designed to help you dive deeper into the transformative practice of generosity. Through this guide, you can uncover personal insights and practical applications of generosity, not just as an action but as a way of life that enriches both the giver and receiver. The benefits are spiritual and practical: You will learn how generosity can lead to greater joy, purpose, and connection with others.

To use the guide effectively, take time to reflect on each question, discuss insights with a group if possible, and consider ways to implement each principle in your own life. By moving through the guide thoughtfully, you will cultivate a more generous, fulfilling approach to life.

The discussion guide is divided into ten sessions, and within each session, there are five sections:

- **Story:** In this section, you will review a specific story from the chapter for inspiration and instruction on generous living.
- **Recap:** The recap reviews a summary of the chapter's big idea.
- **Reflect:** This section is a personal journey, a time to contemplate the truths of how the Holy Spirit is speaking to your heart and mind. Keep this question in mind: *Lord, how are you loving me at this moment to make me more like your Son and my Savior, Jesus Christ?* And you'll find yourself drawn closer to the topic of generosity and its spiritual implications.
- **Prayer:** Take time to pray. In your conversation with the Father, Son, and Spirit, listen for divine affirmation and guidance.
- **Practice:** These questions will help you discover where and how the Lord is leading you to put into practice what he is teaching you. Consider what your next step will be on your journey of generosity.

Session 1

Prologue, Preface, and Introduction

Story

What spoke to your heart and inspired your imagination from Jonathan and Callie Rich's story?

What spoke to your heart and inspired your imagination from Grandmother Smith's story?

What spoke to your heart and inspired your imagination from the modern Macedonian story?

Recap

You experience God in the great adventure of generous living.

"As Jesus taught, freedom and fulfillment come only by giving our lives away: 'If you cling to your life, you will lose it; but if you give up your life for me, you will find it' (Matthew 10:39 NLT). At this crossroads of giving our lives away for him, we have discovered the abundant life he has for us. A life that is truly life" (from the prologue).

"God does not need your money, but he does want you. With generous love, Jesus Christ gave himself for you. As you receive God's gift of grace, God calls you to generously give yourself to him to be loved and to love. You first give yourself to the Lord since he has given his all for you" (from the introduction).

Paul instructed the Corinthian Church with the example of the Macedonian believers: "The grace that God has given the Macedonian churches.... They gave themselves first of all to the Lord.... See that you also excel in this grace of giving" (2 Corinthians 8:1, 5, 7 NIV).

Reflect

What did Jesus mean by "If you cling to your life, you will lose it; but if you give up your life for me, you will find it" (Matthew 10:39 NLT)?

How are you experiencing God, or how would you like to experience God in the great adventure of generous living?

What did Paul mean by "The grace that God has given the Macedonian churches.... They gave themselves first of all to the Lord.... See that you also excel in this grace of giving" (2 Corinthians 8:1, 5, 7 NIV)?

How are you experiencing God's grace by giving yourself first to him and by excelling in the grace of giving?

Prayer

Generous Lord, show me your heart for me as I journey with you in a life of generosity. Show me what it looks like to give myself to you first.

Practice

How is the Lord leading you to put into practice generous living?

How is the Lord leading you to totally surrender to him by excelling in the grace of giving?

Session 2

Chapter 1: God's Generous Love

Story

What spoke to your heart and inspired your imagination from the story of being fully known and fully loved by a parent?

Recap

"C. S. Lewis described how God pursues us, his creation. God is the wooer, and we are the wooed: 'Our highest activity must be response, not initiative. To experience the love of God in a true, and not an illusory form, is therefore to experience it as our surrender to His demand, our conformity to His desire'"[75] (from chapter 1).

Reflect

What did Lewis mean by "Our highest activity must be response, not initiative?"

How are you experiencing God's love as he patiently and graciously pursues you?

Prayer

Loving, heavenly Father, show me how you love me in my current season.

Practice

How is the Lord leading you to experience his pursuing love?

75 C. S. Lewis, *The Problem of Pain* (HarperOne, 2001), 44.

Session 3

Chapter 2: Faithful Manager

Story

How would you describe your intentionality in living for God's kingdom after reading "A Modern-Day Parable of Kingdom Living" at the end of chapter 2?

Recap

Tim Keller described how our view of ownership affects our generosity: "A lack of generosity refuses to acknowledge that your assets are not really yours, but God's."[76] Tim's keen insight describes how God's Word and a generous community call us out to experience the power of generosity through generous living.

Reflect

What did Tim mean by "Your assets are not really yours, but God's?"

"Everything in the heavens and on earth is yours, O Lord" (1 Chronicles 29:11 NLT). How is the Lord's ownership of all you have influencing your generosity decisions?

What does it look like in your life to be rich toward God?

Prayer

Generous God, show me your heart for all you have blessed me with: relationships, time, money, assets, and influence.

76 Timothy Keller, *Generous Justice: How God's Grace Makes Us Just* (Dutton, 2010), 91.

Practice

How is the Lord leading you to celebrate his ownership of all that you have?

Session 4

Chapter 3: Diligent Sower

Story

What spoke to your heart and inspired your imagination from the story of Elver and his crew working diligently to prepare the soil by removing obstacles, plowing, and overseeding?

Recap

"After explaining the promise of sowing and reaping, Paul described the spirit and attitude we should have in our sowing and reaping: 'The point is this: whoever sows sparingly will also reap sparingly, and whoever sows bountifully will also reap bountifully. Each one must give as he has decided in his heart, not reluctantly or under compulsion, for God loves a cheerful giver' (2 Corinthians 9:6–7 ESV). We are to give cheerfully, not under compulsion" (from chapter 3).

Reflect

What did Paul mean by "Each one must give…not reluctantly or under compulsion, for God loves a cheerful giver"?

What are indicators in your life that you are growing as a cheerful giver?

Prayer

Loving, heavenly Father, show me how you cheerfully give to me daily.

Practice

How is the Lord leading you to grow as a cheerful giver who generously sows seeds of love and life for the Lord?

Session 5

Chapter 4: Beyond Blessed

Story

What spoke to your heart and inspired your imagination from the story of the Bell family and their multigenerational generosity?

Recap

"Gratitude is a natural launching pad for generosity....Gratitude is being thankful for what God has done through the generous gift on the cross of his son, Jesus Christ, who, by grace through faith, offered you salvation and refreshed you with forgiveness of sin and abundant living....Jesus left the riches of heaven to lift us out of our spiritual poverty so we might experience the riches of his grace and mercy. Gratitude for his indescribable, generous gift compels us to generous living!" (from chapter 4).

Reflect

"You know the grace of our Lord Jesus Christ, that though he was rich, yet for your sake he became poor, so that you by his poverty might become rich" (2 Corinthians 8:9 ESV). How did Jesus become poor so you might become rich?

What are the riches you experience when you experience Jesus Christ's abundant life?

Prayer

Loving, heavenly Father, reveal your desire for me to use your grace to grow a heart of gratitude that expresses itself in gracious generosity.

Practice

How is the Lord leading you to grow a heart of gratitude that bears the fruit of generous living?

Session 6

Chapter 5: Creating Sacred Spaces

Story

Beth Bennett experienced her own season of spiritual exhaustion from serving others before she leaned into silence and solitude. What elements of her story resonate with your heart, and how do you need to give yourself permission to create more sacred spaces for your soul?

Recap

Henri Nouwen spoke with the authority of truth when he said, "Solitude is not a solution. It is a direction. The direction is pointed to by the prophet Elijah, who did not find Yahweh in the mighty wind, the earthquake, the fire, but in the still, small voice; this direction, too, is indicated by Jesus, who chose solitude as the place to be with his Father."[77] Indeed, moving toward solitude is the Spirit's path of intimacy.

77 Henri Nouwen, "Open Yourself to the Great Encounter," Henri Nouwen Society, March 17, 2024, https://henrinouwen.org.

Reflect

How did Elijah experience God's still, small voice in 1 Kings 19:11–12?

Ponder and pray over Psalm 46:10: "Stand silent! Know that I am God!" (TLB). What does this look like in your current season of being loved by and loving the Lord?

Prayer

Father of all comfort and great mercy, show me by your Holy Spirit what sacred spaces look like in my life so my soul can be refreshed by you to refresh others.

Practice

How is the Lord leading you to invest in essential times of solitude and silence so that you can discern and trust him in the nonessentials (activities that may be good but not the best)?

Session 7

Chapter 6: Being Relationally Intentional

Story

As you read about Charlie Renfroe's seventy-fifth birthday celebration, what came to your mind and heart about the intentionality of his lifetime of relational investments? What fruit did he and his wife, Patty, experience during his milestone birthday celebration?

Recap

"The quality of our lives is determined by the quality of our relationships. Who we spend time with is who we become" (from chapter 6).

Reflect

What are the implications of Proverbs 13:20: "Walk with the wise and become wise, for a companion of fools suffers harm" (NIV)?

How are you generously reserving time to be available for those who will sit in the reserved section of your funeral?

Prayer

Heavenly Father, I am so grateful for your generous relational access, which allows me to celebrate my joys, grieve my sorrows, and grow in the likeness of your love. Reveal to my heart your heart for increasing the quality and quantity of our time together.

Practice

How is the Lord leading you to generously invest time, wisdom, and resources in those he brings into your life?

Session 8

Chapter 7: Serving Humbly

Story

How were you inspired by the story of Jay and Tracy Arntzen's model of humility as they went through the process of discerning God's heart in what broke their hearts, resulting in a ministry to orphans?

Recap

"Humility is the first step to a generous life. It serves as the foundation to build on as we seek to apply our Lord's more challenging teachings of turning the other cheek, praying for and loving our enemies, and defending the sanctity of marriage, to name a few. Without the foundation of humility, Jesus' beatitudes, which are statements of blessing, can feel burdensome and unachievable. But lived out with a spirit of humility, they are life-changing and compelling arguments for generous living through the power of Jesus Christ" (from chapter 7).

Reflect

How is humility the first step to a generous life?

What does it look like to 100 percent surrender to God and then generously give yourself to serve God?

Prayer

Humble Jesus, you became poor so that I might experience true riches in you. You became a servant of no reputation so that I might follow your example. Show me what it looks like to willingly wash others' feet in humble service to others in your name.

Practice

Where and how does God want you to stop engaging in less important activities and start engaging in more meaningful service with kingdom impact?

Session 9

Chapter 8: Living Generously

Story

Clayton and Emily Edward's story included crafting a generous living mission statement: "We strive to maximize our gifts, opportunities, and relationships to further God's kingdom as we raise three amazing children and love each other unconditionally. We are faithful stewards of our time, talent, and treasure. We create fertile ground for the gospel and encourage others in Christ as we serve our family, friends, and community." Pray about, ponder, and draft a generous living mission statement.

Recap

"Proverbs 3:5, which says, 'Trust in the Lord with all your heart, and do not lean on your own understanding' (ESV), is a well-recited truth in the Christian life. Many have used this reassuring verse as a go-to when approaching God, anxious as they stare down an unsure future or grapple with a hard decision. Yet the precise context of this proverb describes a faith-focused life around trusting and honoring the Lord with our resources" (from chapter 8).

Reflect

What does it look like to totally trust the Lord with your resources so that they reflect his ultimate ownership?

Ask the generous community of Father, Son, and Spirit to reveal to you the generous community you are being led to facilitate and follow the Spirit's guidance to nurture and thrive.

Prayer

Generous Jesus, you lived a generous life, which has led me into the great adventure of following you. Show me what it looks like for me to follow you generously in this season of my life.

Practice

What does the impact of generous living look like for you now and in the future?

Session 10

Epilogue

Story

"Electric vehicles are quiet, dependable, and powerful as long as they have received a proper charge. After 250 to 350 miles, a driver must stop and recharge to continue driving. The same is true for the power of generosity at work in your life" (from the epilogue). How does the process of being empowered by the Holy Spirit look like the process of charging an electric car?

Recap

"Moment-by-moment surrender to the Spirit is the spiritual charge that you need to experience the riches of God's generosity, which empowers and motivates you to radical generosity. Generosity becomes as natural as breathing as you inhale the Spirit's power and exhale competing desires. Humility helps you stay plugged into the power of the Holy Spirit" (from the epilogue).

Reflect

How does humility help you to stay plugged into the power of the Holy Spirit?

In John 16, Jesus promised that once he ascended to heaven, he would send the Holy Spirit to guide us in truth (v. 13), to glorify Jesus, and to give to us what is the Father's and the Son's (v. 15). That is generous indeed! How is the Holy Spirit empowering you for generous living?

Prayer

Sweet Holy Spirit, empower me with your love and compassion to discern wisely when you are leading me to be generous with the time, resources, and wisdom you have given me. Make me a vessel of your love and purposes so that God is glorified and all are drawn to Jesus. Show me your heart of generous love for me so that I might share a generous heart of love with others.

Practice

What is the Lord saying to you through this prayer in his Word?

> For this reason I bow my knees before the Father, from whom every family in heaven and on earth is named, that according to the riches of his glory he may grant you to be strengthened with power through his Spirit in your inner being, so that Christ may dwell in your hearts through faith—that you, being rooted and grounded in love, may have strength to comprehend with all the saints what is the breadth and length and height and depth, and to know the love of Christ that surpasses knowledge, that you may be filled with all the fullness of God.
>
> Now to him who is able to do far more abundantly than all that we ask or think, according to the power at work within us, to him be glory in the church and in Christ Jesus throughout all generations, forever and ever. Amen. (Ephesians 3:14–21)

Acknowledgments

Rita, my wife, best friend, and lover, models generosity daily with her beaming smile, attentive listening, and patient questions. Oh, how she gives all of herself to everyone who knows her. Her superpower is making you feel safe, known, understood, and loved.

A big shout-out to Jessica Pollard, editor at BroadStreet Publishing. Jessica patiently read every word in this book more than once, assuring clarity, smooth transitions, and readability. And most impressive was her gracious spirit when making corrections and suggestions. I'm beyond blessed and grateful for Jessica's professional and prayerful investment in these writings.

Four groups of men have generously poured into me for many years: our sons-in-law, Todd, Tripp, JT, and Tyler; our Finishing Well accountability group, Woody, Frank, Scotland, and Mike; our Buckhead book club, David, Nathan, and Mike; and our Cottage book club, Bill I., Larry, Kevin, and Bill W. Thank you, men, for making me a better man who follows Jesus.

Andy and Jodi, Bill and Alison, Josh and Aria, and Jason and Nisae, for over a dozen years in our life group, you have provided a safe environment to nurture my marriage with generous love, vulnerability, and accountability, which helped Rita and me lean into growing a healthy marriage. Thank you, precious friends, for your generous agape.

Our NCF Georgia team—Patti, Maureen, Matthew, Debra, Becky, and Angie—wakes up every day to systematically create environments to inspire biblical generosity for God's kingdom. I'm so grateful for your generous service and love for God's beloved givers.

Our Wisdom Hunters team—Rita, Wendy, Glencora, Rachel, Tripp, Susan, and Rachel—generously shares God's unchanging truth in our ever-changing world. Thank you for generously sowing God's Word into hungry hearts so they can go deeper in their love relationship with Jesus.